The Sacred Path of Peace

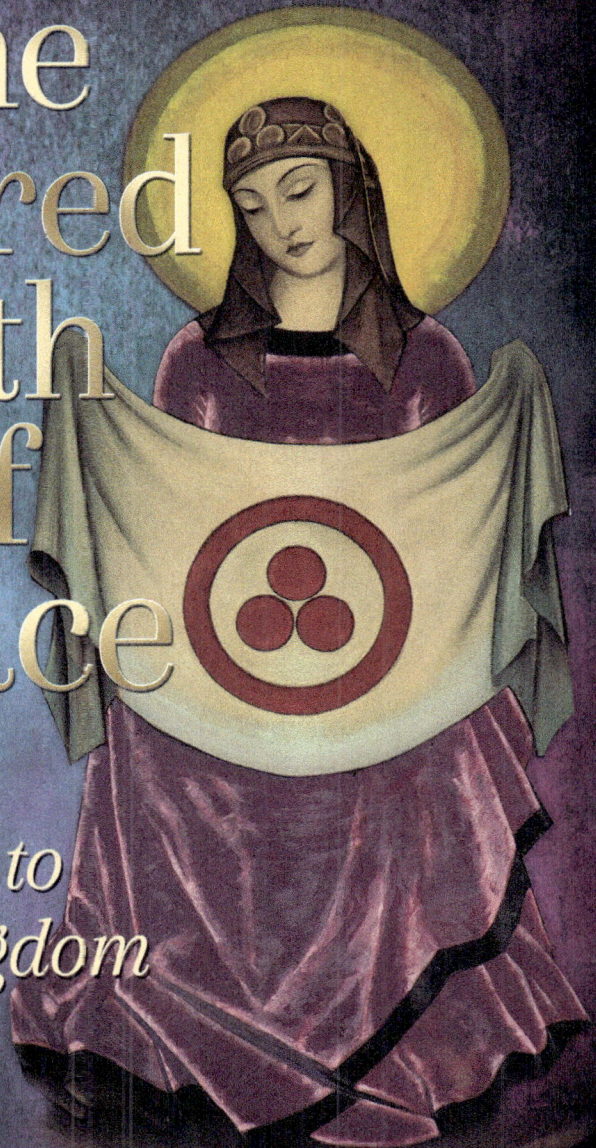

*Keys to
the Kingdom*

Jaya Sarada

Divine Light Publishing

P.O. Box 1110

Gleneden Beach, Oregon 97388

1.855.505.3935

TheTranscendentPath.com

Copyright 2018

All rights reserved.

Cover & Interior Design by: Dianne Rux - D'ziner Graphics

diannedziner@gmail.com • www.dzinergraphics.com

ISBN 9781893037-23-6

Library of Congress Control Number: 2018900632

DivineLightPublishing.com

TheTranscendentPath.com

The Sacred Path of Peace
Keys to the Kingdom
©2018

Cover and Interior Photo Credits:

"Madonna Oriflamma," Tempera on canvas, 1932, front cover art., and
"The Mother of the World" sketch, Banners of the East series, 1924, back cover art,
Courtesy of the Nicholas Roerich Museum, www.roerich.org.
Robert Glenn — Roses and Flowers, www.robertglennphotography.com
pixabuy images, Jaya Sarada photogrpahs,
Arielle Beauduy photographs.

The Sacred Path of Peace
Keys to the Kingdom

A Visual Satsang

Deeply transformational and potent messages placed on Sacred photos.

Awakening begins through seeing with our inner eyes and feeling with our hearts. It is our ability to say "yes" to our birthright of Divine being. It is through unity with the Divine, we are truly able to let go of our sense of separation and begin our path of ever-evolving love.

May you be guided on your inner journey to realize your true nature.

Om Shanti, Shanti, Shanti

Peace be with you

The Sacred Path of Peace
Keys to the Kingdom

Received by
Jaya Sarada

Jaya Sarada grew up in Ojai, California. Her mother, Marjorie Keller was a devout Theosophist and student of Krishnamurti as well as other teachings of truth. Jaya, along with her brother, Brad and sister, Sandhya, were deeply blessed to be immersed in these teachings.

Jaya journeyed to India many times with her family to explore the spiritual culture of India. Her quest for truth began at an early age and continued to deepen throughout her life. She passed these blessings onto her daughters, Alyssa and Arielle.

Jaya Sarada, brings to her work and writing, years of devotion and service. As a holistic, vibrational healer she has helped many overcome stress and illness. Her gifts as a spiritual counselor and ordained minister offer pathways of truth, light and love for all who receive her guidance.

Jaya is the author of several books on healing and transformation such as *Trust in Yourself, The Path of Return, Living Meditations, Sacred Kinesiology, Life Essence Awakening, and Awakening Your Chakras.*

Her work, *The Sacred Path of Love-Communion with God* and *The Sacred Path of Peace-Keys to the Kingdom,* are treasured books that offer love and guidance for those seeking self-realization.

With the understanding that the soul has many facets, like a diamond, Jaya assists her readers and students to awaken to the gifts of their being. These gifts act as guide post to remember your soul's origin and they are felt and understood by accessing the higher frequencies of love, light and truth. We are on the forefront of a new humanity. It is a time in our soul's development where each individual is being called to bring forth what is true and real inside. We are guided to listen to our inner calling and match the miracle of life that we feel inside through the expression of deep

gratitude, joy, love and service. Jaya offers guidance on how to tap into the magnificent being that you are, how to feel awake, alive and full of vitality, how to reconnect with your true nature, and how to discover your unique soul's purpose. During this time of evolutionary awakening we are guided to take a step into our Divine potential. Jaya invites you to take this step and enter the temple of your inner light, where you are simply asked to let go of all that is prohibiting you from experiencing your radiant self.

To learn more about Jaya's work please visit TheTranscendentPath.com.

5

Precious friends who helped with the creation of this book

I am eternally grateful to Dianne, Patricia, Marcia and Arielle for assisting in bringing this book to manifestation.

My deepest gratitude to Dianne Leonetti-Rux, who has brought this book and all my books into reality. Your creativity, beauty and love is truly felt and seen in everything you do.

Thank you, Patricia, my lifelong friend for devoting your love, care and attention to refine the messages received in this book.

And much gratitude to Marcia for writing down the Sacred messages, a service of great love that will help many souls in awakening.

I am so very grateful to my daughter, Arielle who has played a profound role in the creation of this book.

Eternal love and gratitude to my partner and best friend Tom Clarke, who has been the light and support behind all my work.

You are all dearly loved and will always be in my heart.

Blessings

I honor the place in you in which the entire universe dwells.
I honor the place in you which is of love,
of truth, of light and of Peace.
When you are in that place in you,
and I am in that place in me...
We are one.

Gratitude is a way of being, a path that leads us to growth,
joy, abundance, love and resonance with the universe.
Gratitude is a prayer that is cultivated within our hearts and
inspires us to give back to life, the many gifts that we receive.
Gratitude leads us to view life as precious and to understand
that life has nurtured us to our fullest potential. For this we give
thanks by offering life our love, compassion, joy and service.
Whether you are a dear friend, a Sacred sister, a family member,
a teacher or have been a team member in these book creations,
you have been a key part of the evolution of my life and work.
I want to express my deep gratitude to all who have crossed
my path and shared with me this Sacred journey of life.

Namaste
Jaya

Contents

*In devotion to the Loving Creator
of all life and the guidance
of his Council of Light.*

Divine Teacher Transmission

The Blessing for this Work
Received by Jaya Sarada

Seek the Kingdom first and you will know God.

The gift of seeking the Kingdom is found in the heart of humans that have opened to their Divine Source. The wisdom gained through seeking the Kingdom is to understand the nature of reality. This understanding leads to a life with true meaning and purpose.

When you take the path toward the Kingdom, the Holy Spirit holds your hand on your journey home. With the Holy Spirit you will know truth, and Divine love that can never be experienced through the mind.

The inner life of one who seeks the Kingdom is at Peace. Peace is lived as a devotional prayer to God.

**The journey to the Kingdom is paved with
truth, grace, beauty and great love.**

This life is so very precious. It is an invitation to use the physical body as a vehicle for return and to remember who you are.

Peace is of the heart, not of the mind.
To know Peace you have to
find out what beauty is.
The way you talk, the words you use,
the gestures you make, these things
matter very much, for through them
you will discover the refinement
of your own heart.
Beauty cannot be defined, it cannot be
explained in words. It can be understood
only when the mind is very quiet.

J Krishnamurti

The Phoenix Rising

The Phoenix is a legendary bird which is said to periodically burn itself to death and emerge from the ashes as a new phoenix, a symbol of life, death, and rebirth.

The Phoenix is represented here as the metaphor for our soul, a symbol of eternal life. As we walk on this earth at the same time we live in the heaven realm. When Divine love awakens within our soul, the bindings of the past are released and we are renewed in spirit. Our hearts are liberated from the effects of the egoic self and we are united with the Holy Father.

This process is the time when true service begins. The Holy Father or Divine Consciousness becomes the charioteer in our life and the ego is the chariot used by God to travel to the Kingdom. As children of God, we claim our birthright of eternal freedom, joy and Peace.

Asato ma sad gamaya
Tamaso ma jyotir gamaya
Mrtyor ma amritam gamaya

Lead us from non-being to being
Lead us from darkness to light
Lead us from death to immortality

Om Shanti, Shanti, Shanti

Introduction
The Life of a Soul in a Human Body~The Journey Within

The introduction to this work is to understand what it means to be a soul in a human body. The energetic anatomy of a soul is one that has within its blueprint an emotional, mental and spiritual body. These are the components of a soul's vehicle.

At the beginning of awakening, one will become interested in seeing the truth of wholeness rather than identifying with the limited parts of one's energy anatomy; the body, mind and emotions. Within this human conditioning we identify with the body as the nature of our self, or we believe our emotions or thoughts constitute our true reality. This identification is what causes fragmentation of our soul. Underneath all thought and emotion is the feeling body; our pure being that is in direct relationship to life.

Souls come and go in the world. This is a part of creation. All souls have within their heart a spark of God. There is a light that lives within all hearts. Each soul has the invitation to activate this light, but many choose not to awaken due to past life karma. The pain from unhealed lifetimes is held within the memory of a soul and must be felt for a soul to truly awaken. Within the core of most souls lives this unhealed pain caused by separation from their Divine Source. The result is a deep feeling of unworthiness, a veiling of inner light. God will never extinguish this light in a soul. This most Sacred light will never die as it was never born. It is the all-encompassing eternal light of God.

God dwells in you, as you, and you don't have to 'do' anything
to be God-realized or Self-realized.
It is already your true and natural state.
Just drop all seeking, turn your attention inward,
and sacrifice your mind to the One Self radiating in the heart of your very being.
For this to be your own presently lived experience,
Self-inquiry is the one direct and immediate way.

Ramana Maharshi

Peace
The Foundation For Your Awakening

When you feel a Peaceful joy, that's when you are near truth.

Rumi

Belonging to the Kingdom, you came from Peace and you will return to Peace. This is the Peace of the Holy realm. To know this Peace, you must learn to rest in the silence of your Divine heart. Turn within and gently guide the mind to relax into the stillness of your being. In your inner temple the gifts of truth, love, and grace are bestowed upon you.

When you identify with yourself as a separate individual with the story of you, the history of you, there is a lack of Peace due to fear and sorrow. When you begin to let go of the thought of yourself as a separate entity in time, you expand your consciousness to your timeless grace. This letting go awakens the feeling body within and you begin to commune with your inner true nature. Peace becomes the foundation for your awakening.

Through Peace you recognize your inner being, free from your story, and free from the patterns of thoughts or emotions. Mistaken identification is the result of a lack of Peace. When there is Peace, there is stillness and there is only consciousness. Most beings have not experienced true Peace as they are always seeking something to define who they are. When Peace is present, all seeking stops.

Sanat Kumara

Beloved Holy Teacher of the highest dimension,
director of the *Great White Brotherhood,*
we are eternally grateful for your love and devotion
to healing the darkness of this planet.

Your Divine teachings have graced this book for all
to receive your light and guidance toward soul initiation.

The Hierophants, Lord Maitreya and Lord Sanat Kumara,
are guiding us to our awakening in truth, love, and beauty.

They serve to bring us an era of Peace, Love and Harmony.

I bow to you in service and complete surrender
to bring about your teachings to the world.

With great love,

Jaya Sarada

The beauty you see in me,
is a reflection of you.

Rumi

Dedicated to the Holy Council of Light
and the wisdom that is presiding
over the awakening
of Divine Consciousness.

Lord, make me an instrument of thy Peace.
Where there is hatred, let me sow love,
Where there is injury, pardon;
Where there is doubt, faith;
Where there is despair, hope;
Where there is darkness, light;
And where there is sadness, joy.

O Divine Master, grant that I may not so much seek
to be consoled as to console,
to be understood as to understand,
to be loved, as to love.

For it is in giving that we receive,
It is in pardoning that we are pardoned,
and it is in dying that we are born to eternal life.

St. Francis of Assisi

Love is Living in the Heart of God

The love of God is the infinite expression of *Divine* radiance showering you with blessings of grace and guidance in your life. This is directly experienced in the hearts of those who are open to receive *this supremely Holy* grace.

The life of one who lives with the heart of God is never alone.

There is always a feeling of a Holy presence that is with you each moment.

This moment
This love
comes to rest in me,
many beings in one being
In one wheat-grain
a thousand sheaf stacks.

Inside the needle's eye
a turning night of stars.
This moment —
This love.

Rumi

Key of Light
*Peace is born from silence, emptiness
and freedom from the Self.*

Sacred Practice ~ Cultivating Peace

Begin your day by choosing Peace. Have the intention to live each moment in Peace. This is true devotion. You are a precious being of God that is always worthy of Peace. You simply must choose it; that is all that is required. Peace then lives within you as a guidance for your life. It teaches you to mindfully walk on your path with Peace as your companion.

Mistaken identification is a source of conflict. Through the art of letting go of the past you open yourself to the highest teachings of Peace. This is the dimension of true healing that heals the effects of sorrow and separation from God. Peace is the presence of God within your heart. This is the most important attribute that is needed to begin the awakening process.

Be at Peace first; then ask for self-understanding and self-realization.

This step is necessary to truly find God.

You must become still so the voice of God can be heard. The test of your soul is to enter the Kingdom with an open heart and a restful mind. This will become a familiar step as you evolve in your spiritual awakening.

Freedom from sorrow is living in the Peace of the Holy Spirit found within your Sacred heart.

Deep inside of each one of us
is light that is utterly peaceful and quiet.

It is the you in me and the me in you.

It is unaffected and undisturbed
by the outer world.

It is unchanged by birth and death.

It is not limited by time and space.

Teachers can teach you about the world,
but only you can come to know the inner you.

This inner light is always pure,
ever present, and free of sorrow.

Learn to rest in the Self.

Come to know the Bliss.

Sage Vashishta

(Vashista is the Son of God Brahma)

As forgiveness allows love to return to my awareness,
I will see a world of Peace and safety and joy.

Course in Miracles

Wisdom is the Understanding of Truth

The mind is like a child that is in resistance to what is present now. The wisdom to see the truth is naturally present when the mind is still. To live in wisdom is to live within your Sacred heart.

Spend moments of your day to journey deep into your spiritual heart; breathe, rest and renew in this eternal wellspring.

This is your soul's journey of greatness; to know God and to meet God within your Sacred heart.

Enter the cave of your heart and open to the void of your being.

Within this cave you will be transformed by the Sacred energy there. It is through seeking the Kingdom that you will be guided to your inner truth.

Peace on earth is the awakening of each soul in the light of truth ~ Peace within all beings is letting go of self-afflictive sorrow.

The way of Peace is through love ~
The way of love is through Peace.

When another person makes you suffer,
it is because he suffers deeply within himself,
and his suffering is spilling over.
He does not need punishment;
he needs help.
That's the message he is sending.

Thich Nhat Hanh

Key of Light
With love, all things are possible.
With love, we enter the Kingdom.

The disciples said to Jesus,
"Tell us, how will our end come?"
Jesus said,
"Have you found the beginning?
Then why are you looking for the end?
You see, the end will be where the beginning is.
For those who stand at the beginning:
will know the end,
and will not taste death."
Gospel of Thomas

Mathew 6:33

But seek ye first the Kingdom of God, and his righteousness;
and all these things shall be added unto you.

Seek The Kingdom First

Your journey home is paved with the light of the Divine. This most holy light guides you from the human realm to the Divine Kingdom. This is your inner place of Peace, where the hidden gifts of your soul lay waiting to be realized.

Grace, the mystery of life, is experienced as a wind softly guiding your soul home.

All that is required is to let go of mental and emotional burdens that have been impressed upon your soul. When you observe the anatomy of your spirit, you may see that your mind has the habit of projecting fear into the unknown and your emotional body holds the pain of the past. This karmic cycle keeps you from fully experiencing the now, where true Peace is realized.

The way of the new human is to know the truth of being, without the obscuration of thought. You are a being of great light, and can now become the master of your mind and emotions.

Healing will occur when you witness your life from your soul of light.

Welcome this light of the Divine to uplift you beyond the human condition. Understand that the resistance to be free is rooted in the misidentification of yourself as a separate individual self.

As you enter the unknown mystery of your being, you meet the life force within that is free from all conditioning.

And the Peace of God,
which passeth all understanding,
shall keep your hearts and minds
unified with Christ.

Key of Light
In prayer the mind rests,
and the heart opens to its Divine Source.

Sacred Practice
Entering the Inner Kingdom

Seek the Kingdom first and you will know the truth of being. Give up the identification of yourself as a separate self, for you are not one self. You are a unified being with all of creation.

With this understanding there is great love and great service.

The time in a body is for you to realize that you are a Divine being. Your awakening is for the benefit of all humanity. This is understood through the realization that the consciousness of humanity is evolving into a unified consciousness in the next dimension.

There is no separation from your Divine Source.

The powerful calling to remember, is God bringing you home.

Meet your own self.
Be with your own self,
listen to it, obey it, cherish it,
keep it in mind ceaselessly.
You need no other guide.
As long as the urge for truth
affects your daily life,
all is well with you.
To rise in consciousness from
one dimension to another,
you need help.
The help may not always be in the
shape of a human person,
it may be a subtle presence,
or a spark of intuition,
but help must come.
The inner Self is watching and waiting
for the son to return to his father.
At the right time
he arranges everything
affectionately and effectively.

Nisargadatta Maharaj

Perfect love casts out fear.
If fear exists, then there is not perfect love.
But, only perfect love exists.
If there is fear,
it produces a state that does not exist.
Believe this and you will be free.
Only God can establish this solution,
and this faith is His gift.

Course in Miracles

Begin Anew

It is a beautiful time when your mind becomes free from the imprints of the past or the habit of projection into the future. In the Sacred moment of now you stand at the beginning. You will know God.

In timeless moments your light shines bright, and love unifies your soul with all of creation.

You begin to see clearly and the Divine law of truth will be activated in your life. Daily life becomes a communion with God and you sense this Holy presence is with you each moment.

This Holy presence is your guiding force.
Welcome this most Sacred miracle.

Spend moments of your life to sit with this presence with an empty mind and pure heart.

Sacred Practice

Be Still and You Will Know God

Be still within your mind so that the voice of God can be heard.

Live each day with a peaceful mind and you will be shown the way to your infinite being.

The mind that is only concerned with the world is not at Peace for the world is transitory.

The mind that is receptive to the light of God, practices the art of stillness. Through this sacred practice you will know what is eternal, timeless and not subject to change.

Deep within you is a being that is whole and never been touched by the sorrows of this human condition.

Remember to rest in the truth of your being so you may transcend the minds unreality and you will know the infinite light of God.

Father,
I come to You today to seek
the Peace that You alone can give.
I come in silence.
In the quiet of my heart,
the deep recesses of my mind,
I wait and listen for Your Voice.
My Father,
speak to me today.
I come to hear Your Voice in
silence and in certainty and love.
Sure You will hear my call
and answer me.

Course in Miracles

The truth is that
you already are
what you are seeking.

Adyashanti

Key of Light

You stand at the beginning of your innocent nature when
you are empty. This emptiness invites the light of your soul
to shine without imprints that keep you bound to sorrow.
Your mind, when open and free,
can be a mirror of God's light.

The eye through which I see God
is the same eye through
which God sees me;
my eye and God's eye are one eye,
one seeing,
one knowing,
one love.

Meister Eckhart

Sacred Inquiry

The witness of your life is the Divine Consciousness that sees the truth of your life. It is your wisdom eye, the part of you that is free from what is being observed.

This means you see the truth without an investment. Your true nature is pure awareness, witnessing your life just as it is. This awareness is your innate intelligence that guides you on your life path. It is an energy of pure spacious presence, allowing you to be an empty vessel for God's light.

Feel the witness as a waterfall of truth flowing through your being, cleansing and absolving all that is not real. The water purifies your mind and reveals your untouched state of deep Peace.

Key of Light

Rest often in just witnessing. The light is your true nature and through this light you can truly see your mind and the conditioning of your life. In the very noticing of your conditioning, transformation occurs which is the essence of love.

There is a light that this world cannot give.
Yet you can give it, as it was given you.
And as you give it, it shines forth to call you from the world and follow it.
For this light will attract you as nothing in this world can do.

Course in Miracles

Sacred Practice
Living the Question of, "Who AM I?"

Open your mind
to see the truth of your infinite being.
Open your heart
to feel the presence of God within you.
Through self-inquiry you will understand
the light of consciousness.

True Empowerment is Born
When the Ego Dies

Listen within and you will hear the whispers of your true self, the still voice residing in your heart. Your inner wisdom instills within you a deep Peace, and the flowering of acceptance and compassion for your soul's journey. In quiet moments you see that your thoughts and emotions that make up your individual sense of self, are not the truth of your being. Your true self lives before thought, not bound to time and is the source of true empowerment and joy.

The story of your life is an accumulation of time and memory.

When you begin to let go of the story, and its judgements, you will live in forgiveness. Your life force will be free to express in each miraculous moment. This is the beginning of freedom from sorrow. The truth of your being is the unchanging consciousness of grace that guides you through all your changes. The invitation is to rest often in this spaciousness of being, free from the content of the mind.

All of life's experiences can be viewed as an opportunity to build a strong inner temple.

In each experience there is the hand of God assisting you in gaining wisdom and spiritual strength. When you surrender there is movement of the miraculous that manifests and showers you with blessings of the Divine. This Divine force may be the fire of life burning away what is no longer needed in your life. Like the Phoenix you will shed the past to allow something new and unexpected to be born. What a beautiful feeling to let go of the ego self and watch the true unfoldment of life without a doer, a planner, or a sense of being in charge.

In the past paradigm, the imaginary self (ego nature) lives as though it is in control resulting in lifetimes of sorrow due to the consciousness of separation. This separate sense of self is rooted in a false identity, one that fears life and death. When thought is at rest, you will discover a feeling of timelessness and freedom from fear. You are then able to trust that you are letting go into Divine love.

True empowerment is born from letting the ego die so that you may rest in your Divine Source. This is the place where you are filled with the light of the Holy Spirit.

Ask and it will be given to you; seek and you will find;

knock and the door will be opened to you.

For everyone who asks receives; the one who seeks finds;

and to the one who knocks, the door will be opened.

Matthew 7:7

Key of Light

If you bring forth what is within you, what you bring forth will save you.

If you do not bring forth what is within you,

what you do not bring forth will destroy you.

Gospel of Thomas

In the mountain, stillness surges up to
explore its own height.
In the lake, movement stands still to
contemplate its own depth.

Rabindranath Tagore

Be Still and Know That I Am God

Jeshua

Sacred Silence

Sacred silence is the Source of your God Consciousness. This quiet space within is untouched by outward, changing reality. It is realized through turning your attention inward and allowing your mind to fall deep into the sanctuary of your heart. When your mind is at rest you will know Peace and the presence of love.

Begin your journey in consciousness through your inner rest. Let go of the thought patterns that are rooted in survival and your separate sense of self.

Letting go is living life as a prayer.

The inner temple of your heart is where the Divine is felt and can be experienced as a great force that heals your soul and restores your being to innocence. Your wisdom heart realizes that your mind, along with its patterns of thought, is the obstacle that prevents you from awakening to your true self.

Breathe deeply, invite the mind to soften, and your thoughts to fade away as though they are clouds in the sky.

Even those who wish to find happiness and overcome misery

will wander with no aim nor meaning

if they do not comprehend the secret of the mind.

The paramount significance of Dharma.

Shantideva

The journey of a thousand miles
begins with a single step.

Lao Tzu

Love ...

Love makes of each moment an eternity

And tends the garden of the heart's desire.

When love mocks, ruby tears fall heavy as pomegranates

And when love looks, it sees your deepest mystery.

Love seeks out the tears of hidden hearts

And turns not from the Lovers of the Dawn.

Is there a remedy for the pain of love?

Or, is it too unbearable for thought?

One taste of the medicine

And you will realize just how sick you have been.

Those who plead in the defense of love

In love's judgement shall find grace.

And to that court,

May your heart fly...

Hafiz

The way of Peace is the way of love.
Love is the greatest power on earth.
It conquers all things.

Peace Pilgrim

Sacred Practice

Opening Through Silence and Sacred Love

Within you is a love so vast that it cannot be measured. It is always evolving in the Consciousness of God.

Take time to rest in silence so this Sacred love will be nurtured and expressed in the light of truth. This love goes beyond personal love and is an instrument of Divine intelligence that is directly unified with God.

Sacred love will heal the wounds of separation from God and restore you to your original light.

The way of Sacred love is to practice surrendering the content of the personal self. This requires you to live the profound question of, "Who am I?"

When you no longer can answer the question of, "Who am I?", the infinite nature of your being is revealed.

This is what true surrender means.

Go deeper.
Past thoughts into silence.
Past silence into stillness.
Past stillness into the heart.
Let love consume all that is left of you.

Kabir

Opening to the truth of your being
is through silence and Sacred love

The Road to Healing is Through Acceptance & Compassion

Most human beings are deeply wounded from life experiences. The problem is that there isn't a relationship between emotional pain and the healing necessary to release that pain. Emotional pain then lives in the cells of the body and is locked into a pattern of denial that most people hold for their entire lives.

True healing begins when a being can accept everything in their life and through this acceptance release the imbedded painful memories. This rebirth of self occurs through a complete letting go of the past and an emptying of one's heart to be filled by Divine love.

More compassion is needed in this most critical time as humankind lives in great fear and hatred.

When we realize we are the world and our consciousness can bring Peace to this world, we will let go of the inflictions of the ego and our heart will open to greater love, compassion, and acceptance.

Acceptance is an attitude of compassion that seeks to heal others as well as one's self.

We already have perfect compassion,
perfect wisdom, perfect joy.
We only need to settle our minds
so they can arise from deep within us.
Develop the quiet, even state of mind.
When praised by some
and condemned by others,
free the mind from hate and pride,
and gently go your way in Peace.

Buddha

Sacred Practice

Compassion Through Acceptance

The essential truth is that you are a child of God, and within your heart lives the light of pure Divine consciousness.

The story of the human condition is that most people live in fear and therefore are in a state of violence. This is a root cause of suffering. The problem is there is a fundamental mistake in the heart of those who have inflicted pain or have been wounded by others.

Wisdom is to see that all violence and sorrow is one of mistaken identification. The belief that you are a person with a history is the mistake. The mind holds onto this identification to perpetuate sorrow and repeat the patterns of violence. The mind when identified with the personal self, seeks to serve the personal self and sustain its problem nature.

If you let go the of the content of the mind, the light of your being will be revealed. You will then see through this veil of ignorance that has inflicted pain on others and has inflicted pain in your life.

Compassion, the seed of unity, blossoms when there is complete surrender to your Divine Source. Your personality nature no longer controls your life as you remain simply surrendered to the Divine. You live as a chalice of Sacred love, to be used in service to awakening consciousness. The self that was derived from memory dies along with its fear.

Your true nature is born and you enter the doorway to the Kingdom, your home of eternal Peace.

If the doors of perception were cleansed,
everything would appear to man as it is ...
infinite.

William Blake

Peace of mind is clearly an internal matter.
It must begin with your own thoughts,
and then extend outward.

A Course In Miracles

The Blessings of Grace

The mind when one with your true nature, welcomes the stream of well-being. It is open and receptive to the truth. This mind when unified with your heart is free to act with its innate Divine intelligence. It is through the awakening of your Sacred heart that you will become the master of your mind.

Release the hold of the mind; let go and experience grace in your life.

This grace will bring you an ease of being, where you are free to be, free to soar into your infinite potential. The grace of God is the very breath you breathe.

When your mind is resistant it is rooted in fear, which prevents you from experiencing the joy and Peace of your true self. The mind is programmed to keep you elsewhere, in the future or the past. It resists the present moment at all costs, for it cannot provide its function of separation if you are truly in presence, your true self.

The present moment is the doorway to the Kingdom of heaven.

When you walk through this mystical doorway with a surrendered mind, you enter the heavenly realm of everlasting Peace and love.

When you are willing to release the grip of the mind, you cultivate a way of being that allows you to experience the grace that is always present.

This way of being is one of openness, surrender, willingness, and devotion to the heart of God.

The inspiration to evolve Spiritually is already a manifestation
of the presence of God within, and it's certainly indicative of good karma.
Just to want to know truth, to evolve, to improve oneself, to become a better person,
to fulfill one's potential – those are all inspirations.
And the person doesn't make them up; they just come to Him.
It's like an innate desire to fulfill one's potential.
That potential as one evolves becomes more and more identified in Spirituality.
The capacity to love, to forgive, to appreciate,
to see the beauty in all that exists, to live in Peace and harmony instead of discord
and strife, the only requirement is to do whatever you do to the best
of your capacity and leave the rest up to God.

Dr. David Hawkins

Loving Your True Nature

From childhood to old age we embark upon the path of the world's conditioning. In your being, the essence of innocence, we experience life with joy and wonder, living each moment with curiosity. We live in a dream of being without deep conditioning. With time the world's conditioning takes over and we lose our real sense of self. Time-bound, our life energy is molded based on our experiences. We often measure our life according to society's values and spend much of our life trying to become something.

The question now is to ask of ourselves, *"What lives within that is free from conditioning, free from identification? Who is it that lives in this temporary body?"*

In the quiet moments of our day we can pause and contemplate the question of *"Who am I?"* Allowing space and openness to feel the answer. Just living this question will awaken the Sacred light within you.

The mind when empty of thought, thrives on the question *"Who Am I?"* This inquiry guides the mind inward to explore its Source without a definition. This movement of the mind to turn to its Source is the most profound step in self-realization.

Key of Light

The time is now to recover what has been buried

and to uncover what has never been damaged.

This gem of your true nature has always shined in your Sacred heart.

Lay aside all thoughts of what you are and what God is;
all concepts you have learned about the world;
all images you hold about yourself.
Empty your mind of everything it thinks is either
true or false, or good or bad,
of every thought it judges worthy,
and all the ideas of which it is ashamed.
Hold onto nothing.
Do not bring with you one thought the past has taught,
nor one belief you ever learned before from anything.
Forget this world, forget this course,
and come with wholly empty hands unto your God.
The light of the world brings Peace
to every mind through my forgiveness.

Course in Miracles

Sacred Practice

The Courage to See

See the truth of your Divine being, the aspect of you that is always witnessing life's changing experiences. The courage to see is cultivated by realizing your true nature, unaffected by the world of change.

It is within the stillness of your being, your eternal nature receives the courage needed to release identification with the changing nature of reality. This most sacred dimension of consciousness will guide you to transcend the unreal to the real and death to immortality.

The courage to see what true, unaffected by outward experiences is awakened through turning inward and resting in your Sacred heart. In this place of deep Peace, you will naturally surrender all sense of separation from your Divine Source and open to the infinite nature of your being.

Each day is an invitation to spend a few moments and listen to your Sacred heart, so that it may teach you the way of the Divine.

The way of courage is the way of the Divine.

Courage will guide you to take great care of your soul.

Courage will give you the strength needed to let go of attachments.

Courage will assist you to release the past, and hold in your heart the treasures of your life lessens.

Courage will lead you to forgive yourself and others.

The courage of your soul flowers through surrender of separation; it is within the Divine realm of your consciousness that you experience the miracle of life.

That inner Self, as the primeval Spirit,
Eternal, ever effulgent, full and infinite Bliss,
Single, indivisible, whole and living,
Shines in everyone as the witnessing awareness.
That self in its splendor, shining in the cavity of the heart
This self is neither born nor dies,
Neither grows nor decays,
Nor does it suffer any change.
When a pot is broken, the space within it is not,
And similarly, when the body dies
the Self in it remains eternal.

Ramana Maharshi

The Light of Eternity

The road to God is paved with light, truth, beauty, and love. Open to this light and you will be guided home to the Kingdom.

Every step of the way is blessed by grace; you must only keep stepping forward and follow the vibration of God.

The light of eternity is experienced in the quiet space within your heart; the gateway to the heavenly realm. The light of God lives within your Sacred heart and is felt when your mind is at Peace.

This most Sacred force is experienced when you let go of the veil of conditioned existence. In this untouched Holy place within, you will find God and you will be unified with the light of eternity.

Light is love and love is light; in this oneness of God's expression there is heaven.

I have lived on the lip
of insanity, wanting to know reasons,
knocking on a door. It opens.
I've been knocking from the inside.

Rumi

Sacred Practice

Walk in Beauty

The journey to the Kingdom is paved with great beauty and Peace.

Each day you are reminded of God's beauty within this miraculous world.

Each day you are invited to commune with the beauty within your heart and within the hearts of your beloved. This beauty is realized when the mind is in Peace.

Each day is an invitation to see the light in others and light the candle on the altar of your Sacred heart.

Each day is an invitation to listen to the song of your soul which tells you the story of your eternal beauty.

To be beautiful means to be yourself.
You don't need to be accepted by others.
You need to accept yourself.

Thich Nhat Hanh

Freedom of The Personal Self

Soul healing begins when your small ego identity surrenders within to the greater aspect of your being. This letting go is a profound realization that you cannot be defined by the outer world rooted in time. You seek to understand the nature of your true reality beyond the scope of one lifetime. Ask the questions, "What is before birth? What is after death?" This inquiry guides your soul to awaken from the ego's dream. In your contemplation, you will see that any limitation upon your soul has been imposed by thought. Your mind has been enslaved by this conditioned thinking that arose due to the ego's identification based on fear and limitation. Your mind, when reconnected with your Source, is an empty vessel free to experience the eternal nature of your self.

Within you lives a timeless being, a creation of the Divine with only potential as its source. You are free to expand and create as the Divine has created you. You are free to live in an ever-opening state, always receiving more love, light, and joy.

The nature of the personal self is made up of past experiences. When the self lives without inquiring into the truth of these experiences, it dwells in a state of ignorance. This past is imbedded in the self in each new day and it imprisons the innocent being that lives within.

To release the personal self, one must practice true surrender of the false identity that has been formed and claimed by the ego. You have within your heart a great renewing force that will assist you in the practice of letting go of old imbedded images that have been formed from your past experiences. The Divine light of God within you will assist in releasing these untruths and in doing so, your soul will be renewed.

Only humans hold onto these images that are from a self-made mind. The beauty of life is that we can refresh our souls through the seasons of life. Our birthright is to be free, to renew as nature renews. An unfolding flower has roots that are firmly planted in the mother earth. Just like our true nature is soundly rooted in Source, which allows the potential of our being to eternally open to the beauty of our soul.

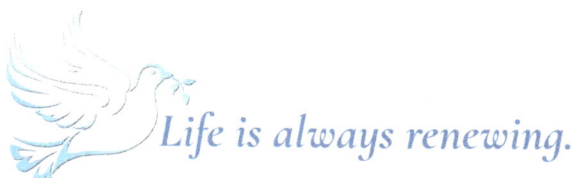

Life is always renewing.

You and I are the same.
What I have done is surely possible for all.
You are the Self now and can never be anything else.
Throw your worries to the wind, turn within and find Peace.

Ramana Maharshi

God dwells in you, as you,
and you don't have to 'do' anything
to be God-realized or Self-realized.

It is already your true and natural state.
Just drop all seeking, turn your attention inward,
and sacrifice your mind to the One Self
radiating in the heart of your very being.

For this to be your own presently lived experience,
Self-Inquiry is the one direct and immediate way.

Every living being longs always to be happy,
untainted by sorrow; and everyone has the
greatest love for himself,
which is solely since happiness is his real nature.

Hence, to realize that inherent and untainted
happiness, which indeed he daily experiences when
the mind is subdued in deep sleep, it is essential
that he should know himself.

For obtaining such knowledge the inquiry '
'Who am I?'
In quest of the Self is the best means.

Ramana Maharshi

Playfully, you hid from me.
All day I looked.

Then I discovered
I was you,

And the celebration
of That began.

Lalla

Precious Guide,

One with all Awakened Ones throughout time and space.

Blissful presence and Source of all spiritual accomplishments,

Fierce destroyer of illusion who dispels every obstruction.

We pray to you for blessing and inspiration.

Please remove all outer, inner and secret obstacles,

And spontaneously fulfill our aspirations.

Author Unknown

Be a lamp, a lifeboat, a ladder,
help someone's soul heal.
Walk out of your house like a Shepard.

Rumi

Grace is always present.
You imagine it as something
high in the sky, far away,
something that must descend.
It is inside you, in your heart.
When the mind rests in its Source,
grace rushes forth,
sprouting as from a spring within you.

Ramana Maharshi

Sacred Practice

The Path of Devotion

Within your heart lives the presence of the Divine and the unlimited capacity to experience infinite love. Through the practice of devotion, you open to this Holy love.

Spend time in your daily life to remember who you are. It is through living your life as a prayer that you experience a communion with each Sacred moment.

In the stillness of your soul you will realize a Divine presence that is discovered through an inner spaciousness of being. This inner spaciousness is Holy light, which is the guiding force of your life.

Embrace the grace of your Divine being as it is guiding you to the Kingdom where you will be restored to wholeness and holiness.

Remember that you are a child of God and you have been sanctified through his Holy light.

The consciousness in you
and the consciousness in me,
apparently two, really one,
seek unity and that is love.

Nisargadatta Maharaj

For a day, just for one day,
Talk about that which disturbs no one
And bring some Peace into your
Beautiful eyes

Hafiz

Self-Understanding~

The Gift of Self-Blessing

Self understanding is the gift of self-blessing that you give to yourself; to love, to know, and to care about yourself as a being of God.

Who are you without your story? What is bubbling under the surface of your conditioning? Look within and you will soon meet your sweet, pure essence that is untouched by the world.

The uncovering of the truth of your being is realized through self- understanding; a gift in which you give yourself. This gift of self love, opens your heart and showers you with Divine light. This is your path of great healing.

The realization of your true self comes from a profound letting go of the false nature of reality. The wisdom to see the false nature of reality is cultivated through silence. The inner eye that intuitively knows the truth must have silence to see clearly.

This world is based on mind-made reality that is seen in time, but the infinite nature of reality is realized through God Consciousness. You are this infinite nature and through surrender you receive your birthright of the realization that you are a child of God. As a child of God the gifts of the Kingdom are bestowed upon you, and you then become a blessing to others.

Sacred Practice

Live Your Life as Prayer

Live your life as though you are talking to God every moment of the day. The mind when focused this way will remain in your Sacred heart and you will know Peace.

This being human is a guest house.
Every morning is a new arrival.
A joy, a depression, a meanness,
some momentary awareness comes as an unexpected visitor...
Welcome and entertain them all.
Treat each guest honorably.
The dark thought, the shame, the malice,
meet them at the door laughing, and invite them in.
Be grateful for whoever comes,
because each has been sent as a guide from beyond.

Rumi

Be your own lamp,
seek no other refuge but
yourselves, let truth be your light.

The Buddha

Joy is the Presence of God

Through opening to your Divine nature, you will experience joy of being. It is different from a happiness that comes and goes with seeking, as an unstable emotion.

Joy is the natural state of harmony with what is present in your life. When you are in joy, you are flowering in God's love.

Joy is the light of your being, which guides you to your soul's purpose. When you follow this joy, you follow the light of God.

Joy is the infallible sign of the presence of God.

Pierre Teilhard de Chardin

Key of Light

Joy is a guiding force that will lead you to Peace
and resolve the conflicts of life.

There is no path to happiness:
happiness is the path.

The Buddha

No matter what chaos appears to be
happening in the world we see,
the most important thing we can do is
maintain a peaceful state of mind.
Our state of mind is always our choice.
We are in complete control.

Course in Miracles

Only the development of compassion
and understanding for others
can bring us the tranquility and happiness
we all seek.

Dalai Lama XIV

God's living grace is your
inner flowering,
mystically created with
your precious souls ever
unfolding beauty.
This beauty has the
Divine fragrance of your
eternal being.

Seeing Through the Eyes of God

For most, life is spent living and seeing through the veil of the conditioned self; our time-bound being. This way of seeing never allows us to see what is true; the eternal reality of our precious life. In our judgments, we see with the eyes of the past and often with a projection onto the future. When what we see in life is filtered through our conditioned mind, our seeing will be limited, fear based, fragmented, and judgmental.

By way of our inner awakening process, we train our mind to return to emptiness.

This emptiness is experienced when there is a deep letting go of the content of our mind and a resting in spacious awareness. It is through our spacious awareness that we are gifted to see through the eyes of God and experience this most Sacred light. We enter the realm of freedom from thought. As we train the mind in this way, we become a vessel of truth, unbound by thought, which will guide our life to Peace.

The invitation from Spirit is to see each precious moment through the eyes of God. This way of seeing will guide us to live life with truth, forgiveness, compassion, and love.

Key of Light

When we see with the eyes of God we can heal what is being seen.
As beings of light, our consciousness holds the truth of God.
We learn the art of true seeing when the mind rests within our heart.

Be a lamp, or a lifeboat, or a ladder. Help someone's soul heal.
Walk out of your house like a shepherd.

Rumi

Transformation of Separation Through Compassion

A personal sense of self is the cause of conflict and harm in the world which results in a great deal of suffering. This mistaken sense of self will unceasingly strive to acquire power through divisiveness because of the nature of its false reality. When we look at the root cause of suffering and conflict in the world, we can clearly see that the core issue is this misled identity, which breeds a serious lack of compassion and love within most hearts.

Human life is now at a crisis in which we must look at:

Why is there no Peace? Why is there so much violence and abuse?

By looking deeper we can see the cause of suffering is self-importance, so much so that we can do great harm to each other. The mistaken sense of self will always think of what is best for its survival and fulfillment of its desires. In the world's conditioning we are programed to think of "I" in all ways: name, image, status, and the illusion of what we think we need to make us happy.

The ego nature must come to an end; a death of this conditioned reality. The way to the end is to see the suffering it has caused in our own life and the collective suffering it has caused in humanity. It is through the awakening of love and compassion within our hearts that the ego nature naturally begins to dissolve.

There must be a greater yearning for something true, real, and a seeking of a love that is not conditioned by the ego's limited and changing desires. The ego will always seek, find, and then discard what has been satisfied, only to seek again, never quenching the thirst for something more.

Transformation is needed to begin the healing of conflict and it begins by releasing the sense of a personal life that is defending itself. When the inner being begins the awakening process, the personal self dies to the story that has bound it to many lifetimes of sorrow.

Key of Light

When we willingly let our ego-self die on the cross of truth,
we experience the Holy light of our soul; the light of God.

When we are motivated by compassion and wisdom,
the results of our actions benefit everyone,
not just our individual selves or some immediate convenience.
When we are able to recognize and forgive ignorant actions of the past,
we gain strength to constructively solve the problems of the present.

Dalai Lama XIV

*Transformation occurs through love of God,
the love of life, and the love of our true self.*

Sacred Practice

Return to Oneness

Within your mind are patterns of thought that prevent you from living in Peace. This is the minds way of perpetuating separation. Beneath the minds activity, lives the stillness of your Sacred heart. Turn your mind toward your Sacred heart and you will meet the Holy one that is guiding you home. This is your true beloved.

Resting in the arms of the beloved is your path to Peace.

Take time each day to practice turning your mind into your Sacred heart, you will soon realize it is your true home.

Within your Sacred heart,
you will journey to the Kingdom.

As I lived up to the highest light I had,
higher and higher light came to me.

Peace Pilgrim

The Divine Flowering of the Sacred Lotus Within

Within the heart of all souls is a Sacred lotus that opens through communion with God. This yearning is a natural expression of the Sacred heart. The lotus within the Sacred heart is uncovered through spiritual activation of Divine love and light. You have the keys to this experience encoded in the very cells of your physical body.

The lotus of your heart is the temple of your soul where God's light is realized.

This inner lotus unfolds through the awakening of the beauty within you. Each petal within the lotus of your heart holds the essence of God.

Each petal is ever unfolding in relationship to your evolution of Divine Love.

Your inner flowering occurs through the upliftment of your being into the heavenly realm. By tending to your inner lotus you cultivate beauty, compassion, joy, goodness, Divine will, truth, and wisdom.

Key of Light

The grace of your inner flowering knows no bounds and eternally unfolds in infinite love, beauty and truth.

The Sacred lotus in your heart will infinitely expand gifting you with heaven's perfume.

All the things that truly matter, beauty, love, creativity, joy
and inner Peace arise from beyond the mind.

Eckhart Tolle

Sacred Practice

Remembering

Life in the human realm is a test to discern the real from the unreal. The wisdom to know the real is your soul's yearning for truth.

The illusionary mind is your soul's test of awakening.

The mind when not examined creates a fictitious sense of self which becomes a veil to your true nature. This covering of your true reality is the seed of great sorrow. Layers of identification with the stories of your life create a deep sense of your personal self based on time and memory. These layers of identification lead to forgetfulness of your true self and a loss of soul vitality. Through inquiry it is possible to pierce the veil that obscures your true nature.

Ask the question "Who Am I?"
and allow this question to dissolve your mind,
into your Sacred heart.

Rejoice in the Grace of Being.

Through contemplation and your sincere quest, the light
of your soul will shine through and you will know God.

Spirit is in a state of grace forever.
Your reality is only spirit.
Therefore, you are in a state of grace forever.

Course in Miracles

I have no name, I am as the fresh breeze of the mountains.

I have no shelter; I am as the wandering waters.

I have no sanctuary, like the dark gods; Nor am I in the shadow of deep temples.

I have no Sacred books; Nor am I well-seasoned in tradition.

I am not in the incense mounting on the high altars, Nor in the pomp of ceremonies.

I am neither in the graven image, Nor in the rich chant of a melodious voice.

I am not bound by theories, Nor corrupted by beliefs.

I am not held in the bondage of religions, Nor in the pious agony of their priests.

I am not entrapped by philosophies, Nor held in the power of their sects.

I am neither low nor high. I am the worshipper and the worshipped.

I am free. My song is the song of the river calling for the open seas.

Wandering, wandering, I am Life.

I have no name, I am as the fresh breeze of the mountains.

J. Krishnamurti

"Heart"
is merely another name for the Supreme Spirit,
because He is in all hearts.
The entire Universe is condensed in the body,
and the entire body in the Heart.
Thus, the Heart is the nucleus of the whole Universe.

Ramana Maharshi

I was Nothing
When my mind was cleansed of impurities,
like a mirror of its dust and dirt,
I recognized the Self in me.
When I saw Him dwelling in me,
I realized that He was the Everything
and I was nothing.

Lalla

Truth is the Divine Law of God

The Divine law of God is instilled in all souls that wish to unite with their true nature. The missing essence for many souls is they do not yearn to know God.

The yearning to know God comes from the wisdom that life is temporary.

The most important understanding is to trust in your life purpose which is complete self-realization. Suffering comes from wanting something more than wanting God; this desire of the personal self is the Source of great unhappiness.

The invitation is to stay in the presence of God throughout all your life. Put all your desires on his altar and rest in surrender.

The bud stands for all things,
even for those things that don't flower,
for everything flowers, from within, of self-blessing;
though sometimes it is necessary to re-teach a thing its loveliness,
to put a hand on its brow of the flower
and re-tell it in words and in touch
it is lovely until it flowers again from within, of self-blessing.

Galway Kinnell

Heaven is Within You

The soul who has found Peace is at the gateway to heaven. This is your journey home.

Heaven is a state of consciousness that is free from self-afflicted sorrow, free from separation from God. This Divine dimension lives within your Sacred heart; It is your true home, your place of Peace and rest, accessible any time through stillness.

Now the calling is perpetual for you to return to your Divine origin.

This calling invites you to live in the world but not of it. Begin by releasing the hold of this world and realize it is passing in time. It is through the realization of the eternal dimension within your heart that you become free from sorrow and unified with your Divine Source.

Joy is your Divine birthright and lives within your heart as the unchanging essence of your true nature. Joy is the light of your being, which guides you to your soul's purpose. When you follow your joy, you are on the path to God. A Divine hand will guide you home and lead you from darkness to the light.

Seek ye first the Kingdom of Heaven because that is
where the laws of God operate truly,
and they can operate only truly since they are the laws of Truth.
A Course in Miracles

Key of Light
Heaven is the place within you
that is found in complete stillness of your being.
Knock and the door will open to you.

A quiet mind is all you need.
All else will happen rightly,
once your mind is quiet.
As the sun on rising makes the world active,
so does self-awareness affect changes in the mind.
In the light of calm and steady self-awareness,
inner energies wake up and work miracles
without any effort on your part.

Nisargadatta Maharaj

Ascending to the Light of God

The Call of the Masters

"We are the masters of the
heavenly realm of timeless being.
We will assist those who are ready to shed their ego body
and ascend to the higher, formless consciousness of God.
You are preparing for heavenly ascension through the release
of what is no longer true for you
and embracing the truth of your Divine being."

Key of Light

Hear the calling and take the path to eternal freedom.
Your path is paved with love, wisdom, beauty,
truth and grace-the gifts of Spirit.

An awake heart is like a
sky that pours light.

Hafiz

Sacred Practice

The Wisdom Within You

Each breath is the gift of God.
Each moment the wisdom within
you is available for you to receive.
Each moment the blessings of
God are with you.

Daily Divine Guidance

Open to the truth of your being.
See the beauty of your soul.
Practice the presence of God.

Be still so you may hear the voice of Spirit that is gently guiding you home.

**Listen to the voice of Spirit and you will be
carried home on the wings of Grace.**

God is one life. Eternal, immortal,
infinite never beginning, never ending.
There is only one God,
therefore, there is only one life.
Practicing the Presence.
Joel Goldsmith

This listening is the art of meditation,
in the learning of which we come to a place
of transition where truth leaves the mind
and enters the heart.
In other words,
there is no longer merely an
intellectual knowledge about truth;
but truth becomes a living thing within our being.

Joel S. Goldsmith

The Field of Being

To willingly enter the realm of stillness within your soul you must surrender what has lived in your identity being. The self that has been created by thought has lived in that made-up identity and is the root cause of your sorrow. What lives within you has never been touched by thought and cannot be defined by what you have been told or what you have told yourself.

The mind has created a play and you are the character in the story.

See this play and the mind-made character as a test for your soul and sincerely realize that it is not true. Your mind along with all if its content does not define your true essence. This powerful realization opens the doorway to your freedom and empowerment. When you walk through the doorway of the conditioned mind you enter the spacious realm of your true being. This is your birthright, your true home, and your heavenly realm of everlasting Peace and joy.

Your heart is the temple of the Divine. It is your source of Peace and joy. It is the gateway to the infinite nature of your being.

It tells you the ancient story of your essential nature which has never been born and will never die. This field of being is your untouched vibration that lives within your heart. Remember your Sacred light as it will guide you in truth.

Key of Light

Trust in your inner field of being to restore your energy
so that you may live in the world without being of the world.

The Way is not in the sky; the Way is in the heart.

Gautama Buddha

Sacred Practice

Infinite Expansion

Most people look to an outer source to find truth, when all along this truth of God lives within your Sacred heart.

Each day of your life is an invitation to commune with your Source. This is a most important time as humanity is in deep sorrow and in need of great healing.

The Holy Spirit lives within your Sacred heart. This understanding is the discovery of a precious gem that shines within you.

Spend moments of each day in prayer, contemplation or meditation. During these precious moments, send love and healing to all who are in need.

Be a blessing to others. Each moment of prayer is a moment of grace that opens you to living in service. Each moment of communion with God is a time to rest in your Sacred heart, and through your rest, when you are in Peace, the gateway to the infinite opens.

Your Sacred heart is your inner place of refuge where you can receive the Divine qualities of God to live in the world, but not of it. It is your inner altar of surrender; through your surrender you receive your soul's gifts.

Peace is the natural state of the mind at its deepest level.
Non-Peace begins in small ways, when you are worried,
restless, distracted, uneasy, or dissatisfied.
Today be mindful of those signals from your inner world.
When you feel them, take a moment to return to your calm space.
Either meditating or simply sitting in a quiet space with eyes closed
and taking easy, deep breaths, works very well.

Deepak Chopra

Surrender is not a weakness.
It is strength.
It takes tremendous strength
to surrender life to the supreme
to the cosmic unfolding.

Mooji

Surrendered Flow

Living in the world's conditioning can be very challenging, as it leads to the belief in separation, fear, conflict, struggles, and identification with the body and mind. Through mental adaptation to the world's conditioning, you learn to function mechanically and then you lose touch with your inner essence.

For lifetimes, many of us have fallen into a state that is not real, into the dream of the mind.

It is the nature of the mind to place you at odds with your essential self. Our environments and relationships nurture our false belief that we are limited, separated individuals. Lifetimes have been lived forgetting the truth. The human condition of old age, sickness and death have no bearing on the light we all share.

God's infinite light is our light and can never be dimmed by any circumstance.

Modern culture rarely places an emphasis on cultivating your relationship with the miracle of God. Very little time is spent nurturing your inner light. Time is an illusion that mistakenly captures your mind into thinking you are a finite person, independent of your Source. When you begin to see more of your light it will reveal to you the mystical truth of life.

Grace unveils your illuminated being when you walk on your path with God.

It is an act of devotion to surrender your changing thoughts and emotions to the Holy Peace within. This will create an opening to the realm of heaven which is your spiritual home.

With God, there is complete fulfillment; this Holy light eternally shines within your heart.

Key of Light

Surrendered flow is like living in a stream of grace.
There is a deep feeling within you of Peace and wellbeing
as you let go of the hold on your personal self.

The practice of stepping back from our perceptions and opening to our right
mind will bring us to the Peace that will guide us through the seeming chaos of the world.
Our true Self will inspire us with right action that quiets fear,
heals our mind and blesses our world.
We can offer no greater gift to the world than to choose Peace first,
moment by moment.
Course in Miracles

Sacred Practice

Living a Surrendered Life

This life is so very precious. You must care deeply for your inner being and practice the art of letting go of thoughts and emotions that have accumulated in your body temple.

*Through your emptiness, you will be filled with God's presence
and you will know Sacred love.*

Surrender, let Silence have you.

Surrender to the Source,
Surrender to awareness,
this is the only place of protection.

Surrender your heart and you will know all.
Surrender to Consciousness and Bliss.
Surrender means to surrender your bondage
and to simply be Freedom.

Papaji

I offer you Peace. I offer you love. I offer you friendship.
I see your beauty. I hear your need. I feel your feelings.
My wisdom flows from the Highest Source.
I salute that Source in you. Let us work together for unity and love.

Gandhi

There is a presence, a silence, a stillness which is here by itself.

There is no doer of it, no creator of this stillness.

It is simply here in you, with you.

It is the fragrance of your own self.

There is nothing to do about this, it is naturally present.

This fragrance of Peace, this spaciousness,

it is the fragrance of your own being.

Mooji

St. Theresa's Prayer

May today there be Peace within.
May you trust God that you are exactly where you are meant to be.
May you not forget the infinite possibilities that are born of faith.
May you use those gifts that you have received,
and pass on the love that has been given to you.
May you be content knowing you are a child of God.
Let this presence settle into your bones,
and allow your soul the freedom to
sing, dance, praise and love.
It is there for each and every one of us.

You Are a Miracle of Life

Life is your Holy gift. It is the miracle of your very breath. You mistakenly think that you are in control of this miracle, when in truth you are God's own creation. This life is your gift from God. Realize you have a living miracle within your Sacred heart. Rest there so you can know the vibration of the Holy one who gave you life.

You do not have a life. You are this miracle of life.

Changeless, formless, you are born of Spirit living in a world of changing appearances. Your eternal spirit lives within the timeless dimension of God. God breathes his Holy love within your soul, giving you the capacity to awaken to your true self.

This is the miracle...
You are eternal Spirit, living in a world of changing appearances.
This is the miracle you truly are.

People usually consider walking on water or in thin air a miracle.
But I think the real miracle is not to walk either on water
or in thin air, but to walk on earth.
Every day we are engaged in a miracle
which we don't even recognize:
a blue sky, white clouds, green leaves, the black,
curious eyes of a child -- our own two eyes.
All is a miracle.

Thich Nhat Hanh

I shall spend every moment loving.
One who loves does not notice her trials;
or perhaps more accurately,
she is able to love them.

St. Bernadette

Sacred Practice

The Healing Breath

The Source of true and long-lasting healing comes from the light of God. You have direct access to this Holy medicine.

Trust in this light to recalibrate your life force,
so that you may be well in your body,
mind and emotions. Practice the art of surrendered breath.

On each exhale let your body relax.
On your inhale, open your arms and reach for the heavens.

Feel the Divine prana entering your out-stretched palms.

Breathe deep and you will soon feel as if you are
being recharged by your Divine Source.

Bring your hands down through your energy bodies,
along your chakras, down your legs and off your feet.

Release anything that is no longer serving you.

Breathe in, and affirm the miracle of your life.

Take time each day to practice this self-care for
your Sacred spirit. You are offering yourself a very
powerful self-healing.

Key of Light

Allow the light to guide you to the healing needed for your soul.

Trust in this light and all will be well.

Timeless Being

Time is a manifestation of this world and not of your true eternal nature. You live within the realm of time, but you are timeless; you are an eternal being of God. The life span in a physical body is time-bound, with birth on one end and death on the other.

The wisdom to see yourself as a never-ending expression of the light of God comes from your true eternal nature.

The way to receive this wisdom is through the quiet mind and by becoming receptive to the voice of Spirit.

Peace of mind is clearly an internal matter.
It must begin with your own thoughts, and then extend outward.
It is from your Peace of mind that a peaceful perception of the world arises.

Course in Miracles

Key of Light
Each day, allow space to feel your inner being that is formless,
timeless and not bound to the world.
Through this feeling you will know God.

Forgiving the Mistakes of Ego Identification

The wound is the place where the Light enters you.
Rumi

Within the human conditioning there is a tendency to believe the content of the mind and emotions define the self. Throughout life the self becomes a prisoner of this identification which is the cause of great sorrow.

The reality of your true essence is an extraordinary miracle. It is the grace of being, which is before thought and deeper then human emotions.

The human condition has caused a superficial sense of separation from God, when in truth you are simply a spark of the Divine

Your Divine Source is your life; the very breath you breathe, the life that breathes you.

To experience lasting Peace there must be a willingness to be humble in relationship to your Divine Source.

Trust in the Divine Source of your life and surrender your mind unto the altar of your Sacred heart. You will then realize that you are simply a child of God. You will awaken to your soul's eternal potential that is evolving in love. Through your surrender you will receive the bounty of the Kingdom, the gifts of truth, beauty and Peace.

Key of Light

Seek the Kingdom before all else and you will know God.
You will be taken home on the wings of your guiding angels.

Go deeper
Past thoughts into silence.
Past silence into stillness.
Past stillness into the heart.
Let love consume all that is left of you.
Kabir

Experience the core of stillness. Dive into it and surrender fully.
In full surrender to stillness, you directly experience that
to which the concept of God points.
In that direct experience, you awaken from the dream of the mind
and realize that concept of God points to who you truly are.

Adyashanti

Sacred Practice

Letting Go

Rest in the truth of your being. Practice the art of letting go of accumulated thoughts and emotions that pretend to define your reality. These tendencies of the personal self are the cause of suffering and a lack of Peace. Seek the Kingdom first by surrendering the habits of the mind that keep you separated from your Sacred Source. The yearning to be free from sorrow opens the path for your journey home.

This is a path of great joy, and on the path you will be guided by angels that are sent by God.

The path is narrow at times and will be difficult as you ascend to higher and higher frequencies, but on each step, you will be elevated through your surrender.

Divine Light will guide you along with your angels to the Kingdom.

The sorrows of duty,
Like the heat of the sun,
Have scorched your heart.
But let stillness fall on you
With its sweet and cooling showers,
And you will find happiness.

Ashtavakra Gita 18:3

Key of Light

You are a light that will never be extinguished.
With Divine grace you will be guided to the truth of your timeless being.

See the Truth and the Truth Will Set You Free

The Origin of Being

Listen: There is within you a Sacred being that is timeless and untouched by life's changing experience. You are the eternal beauty of life whose essence is the ocean but you appear as a wave. You ebb and flow through life's changes but you are always returning to your unchanging true nature. You are the ocean of life with the stories of your soul running as a river, but never effecting the bounty of the sea. Your life is for meeting the truth of your being which is not subject to time. For you are a being that exists before birth and after birth in the eternal flowing river of your soul.

As a being of pure Spirit, you are invited to take your rightful place as a Divine child in the Kingdom. This is your true home of the infinite love and light of the Creator. In your innocent true nature, you enter free from the world's conditioning.

All that is required is that you enter freely without the burden of your separate sense of self.

You are a soul with a light body; your vehicle to explore infinity.

Instilled within your soul is the light of God.

This Sacred light has no beginning,

no end, and is guicing you home to the Kingdom.

Grace

Grace is within you always. It is your breath and the seed of your soul's potential. Grace is the unseen mystery of creation; it is the silent background in which all appears and disappears. It is changeless, formless, and exists in the infinite dimension of your pure consciousness. When you turn within to the silence of being, grace blesses you with her presence of Peace.

Grace is the light of God; this light lives as a Holy presence within your Sacred heart, gently guiding you home to the Kingdom.

Grace brings you the wisdom to transcend your karma so you can use the lessons of your soul as the priceless foundation for your awakening.

Key of Light

Grace is the unfolding of your inner lotus with each petal bringing you the gift of spirit and illuminating your soul as a being of light.

Sacred Practice

Divine Grace Guiding You Home

Grace is always present. You imagine it is something somewhere high in the sky, far away, and has to descend. It is really inside you, in your Heart, and the moment you effect subsidence or merger of the mind into its Source, grace rushes forth, sprouting as from a spring within you.

Ramana Maharshi

Grace is the presence of the Holy Spirit within your heart guiding you home.

Grace is the hand of God that heals your sorrows.

Grace is the wisdom of God that is instilled in your soul.

Grace is the voice of God that leads you to Peace.

Grace is the light of God within your Sacred being.

Grace is the infinite love of God within your heart.

Grace is the willingness to surrender the mind and live in presence of being.

Grace is the voice of God calling you home.

Key of Light

Your Sacred heart is your inner altar where all is surrendered.
The gift of surrender bestows upon your life the blessings of grace.

I believe all suffering is caused by ignorance.
People inflict pain on others in the selfish pursuit
of their happiness or satisfaction.
Yet, true happiness comes from a sense of inner Peace and contentment,
which in turn must be achieved through the cultivation of altruism,
of love and compassion and elimination of ignorance,
selfishness and greed.

Dalai Lama XIV

Your task is not to seek for love,
but merely to seek and find all the barriers within
yourself that you have built against it.

Rumi

Soul Love

In the dimension of Divine Consciousness, your being is unified with God. When you express this aspect of your consciousness you experience joy and give joy back to the Creator. You become a blessing to the world.

As your soul descends into the human realm, your true essence is veiled. Human conditioning sets in and there is a forgetting of who you truly are.

Soul love is the essence of God's love within your heart.

This love is unbound by the personal nature of self; it is the eternal Divine love that lives within your Sacred heart. It holds the intelligence of God. When you are in need of guidance, simply turn within, ask and you shall receive.

Your true essence is a spark of creation that lives in your soul as an ever unfolding potential of Divine Love.

The everlasting expression of this love will always hold you in its Sacred embrace.

Even
After
All this time
The Sun never says to the Earth,
"You owe me."

Look
What happens
With a love like that.
It Lights the whole sky.

Hafiz

Love is the beauty of the Soul.

St. Augustine

Sacred Practice

Soul Love

The realms of consciousness evolve from the base nature of "self" to your highest Divine potential.

Your true nature lives within the vibrational frequency of God and is free from the lower tendencies of "self."

This unity with your Divine source offers you a refuge where your mind can rest and you experience the Peace of the Kingdom.

Meditation

Invite your mind to turn within and rest in the silence of your Sacred heart. Take a few deep breaths so that your body begins to relax.

On each exhale, release the activity of the mind and surrender all to God.

This is your Sacred practice that gives your soul the love and attention that it requires to live in a physical body.

Spend quiet moments in your day to experience the vastness of eternity within your heart.

Love says, "I am everything."
Wisdom says, "I am nothing."
Between the two, my life flows.

Nisargadatta Maharaj,

The Wisdom of Discernment

Compose yourself in stillness,
draw your attention inward and devote your mind to the Self.
The wisdom you seek lies within.

Bhagavad Gita

Wisdom flowers within the unity of mind and heart. When the mind is rooted in deep patterns of identification with thought, a fictitious sense of self develops, and one can spend their lifetime in this illusion. When unquestioned, the mind believes it is a separate entity apart from God. The mind acts mostly as a computer program that follows the dictates of the self. When the self is veiled through ignorance, the mind is veiled as well. To heal the mind, you must live with great discernment.

Awakening naturally occurs when all concepts of self are released and there is a meeting of your true nature that lives within your Sacred heart.

Through your awakening, your mind will be guided to its Divine Source. This is the wisdom that shepherds you to live within the essence of Peace, light, and freedom.

Accept the invitation to turn your mind to God and you will be guided by the wings of grace.

Key of Light

Within your heart of stillness lives the Holy vibration of God.
Through letting go, dropping your mind into your Sacred heart,
a natural healing of separation occurs.
When the Sacred heart is awakened, witness consciousness becomes
the master of the mind and you are no longer bound to thought.
When you become the witness, you break the trance of the mind.
This is the gift of Divine love and grace.

Be patient toward all that is unsolved in your heart and try to love the questions themselves, like locked rooms and like books that are now written in a very foreign tongue. Do not now seek the answers, which cannot be given you because you would not be able to live them. And the point is, to live everything. Live the questions now. Perhaps you will then gradually, without noticing it, live along some distant day into the answer.

Rainer Maria Rilke

Miracles are natural.
When they do not occur something has gone wrong.

Course in Miracles

People have a hard time letting go of their suffering.
Out of a fear of the unknown,
they prefer suffering that is familiar.

Thich Nhat Hanh

Transcendence
Going Beyond Limitation

When asking yourself, "What is transcendence?" there must be a pause in your being; a place within you that falls into silence and waits for the answer. Transcendence means to go beyond thought, beyond the mind into the unknown mystery of life.

What is known is always the past and the new is always a mystery. Transcendence guides you in the process of letting go of accumulated memory that keeps you from living in the present. Transcendence may be understood as a soul art; a way of being in which the mind falls deeper into the empty, healing space of the heart. There is a release of identification with the mind through its merging with the Sacred presence of the heart. Discernment is developed in order to see what is true and untrue. Transcendence deepens your understanding of your precious life force beyond time, beyond conditioning into what is true and never changing.

Key of Light
Through the art of transcendence,
you journey into the infinite plane of being
where you are one with God.

A mind that has understood
the nature of pleasure and fear is
no longer violent and can therefore
live at Peace within itself and
with the world.

Krishnamurti

The unchangeable can only be realized in Silence.
Once realized, it will deeply affect the changeable,
itself remaining unaffected.

Nisargadatta Maharaj

But seek you first the Kingdom of God, and his
righteousness; and all these things shall be added to you.

Matthew 6:3

Sacred Practice

Be a Spiritual Warrior

The Holy Spirit is holding your hand on your journey home.

Remember

You are never alone. Take time to feel the Holy Spirit within you.
It showers you with Peace, joy and

Beauty.

The Holy Spirit envelopes you with grace, blesses you with Divine

Love.

You will know the essence of Peace within the still voice of your

Heart.

This voice of Peace will guide you to your inner temple where you can
let go of the mind and rest. Take time each day to be in

Peace,

allowing Peace to heal all your afflictions.

Be a spiritual warrior and choose Peace first.
Be a light in the world.

Be the light
that shines within you.

The Way of the Courageous Soul

Within your heart lives a light that points to the doorway of the Kingdom. When your yearning for truth awakens you will naturally seek the Kingdom within; the real Source for true and long-lasting happiness and wellbeing. You will naturally begin to surrender the mind and the patterns of sorrow that have weakened your life force.

When you seek the Kingdom first, you become willing to let go of the obstacles on your path toward God. Turning within you meet the essence of your true self and begin to love yourself as a spark of the Divine, a child of God. This meeting of your true self instills a profound respect for yourself as a being of God. Courage to witness the mind is cultivated.

Courage is an aspect of your soul that awakens through yearning for truth. Your intention for truth becomes the arrow and you can see directly into the false nature of the mind. This is a powerful tool of seeing that will set you free.

You must have courage to see the false nature of the mind.

You must understand that what the mind is perceiving is coming from the ego's perspective of separation. When you realize that you are an aspect of God you will no longer need to have an ego identity that impresses upon the mind a belief in the untruth of the personal self. The personal self is imbued with pleasure and pain that are the result of the stories and images created by your mind.

When you experience suffering you relate to the story of pain. When you experience happiness you relate to the story of happiness. What lives within that is untouched by the pain and pleasure of life?

In the core of your being there is only your true essence and the unchanging truth that is not defined by your ego identification. This must be understood for you to be free. It requires great courage to allow the mind to rest in the silence of your heart.

It is a dissolving of the sense of a mind-made self and awakening to the love of being.

This is the way of the courageous soul.

Sacred Practice

Forgiveness

egin each day by offering everything to the loving heart of God. Begin each day with a clean slate erasing the memories that bind you to the past. Feel the grace of your life and receive the lessons of the past. Put them in the crown of jewels in your soul, each jewel being a gift from God.

Know that the light shines always in the darkness of human error, for the error is one of misidentification.

Forgiveness is the healing of the perception of separation.
Course in Miracles

Peace (shanti) is a Divine quality...
One united to "the Peace of God,
which passeth all understanding"
is like a lovely rose,
spreading around him the fragrance of
tranquillity and harmony.

Philippians 4:7

You have to see and meet God in this life.
Don't let this life go by and miss discovering
the Supreme One.
You will find him inside as your constant being.

Pray: Holy mother, Holy father, Holy Spirit,
don't give me the illusion that even
one second belongs to me.
All is you.
I also am you and yours.
For only like this
does your life stand the chance to be miraculous.

Mooji

The Christ in you is very still.
He knows where you are going, and He leads you
there in gentleness and blessing all the way.

Course in Miracles

Knock and He'll open the door.
Vanish and He'll make you
shine like the sun.
Fall and He'll raise
you to the heavens.
Become nothing, and
He'll turn you into everything.

Rumi

Anahata

The Sanskrit name for our energetic heart center is Anahata: "the unstruck sound eternal." Anahata refers to the place within that is untouched by the pain and grief of the materialized world. It resembles an umbilical cord to purity keeping us connected on a deep level to the transcendental. It sings out without having been inspired by something outside us; it sings out because it is our deepest nature.

Forgiveness & Compassion

When the pain of life become too much, our hearts begin to close and there is a tendency to become hardened human beings. We may find ourselves feeling shut down and out of touch with our inner self. We live a life of soul trauma due to the inability to navigate our life story in a conscious manner. This soul trauma can be healed. The invitation from our Divine Source is to return to the wholeness of our being.

How do we turn back to the truth of our being?

When we inquire into the nature of our existence, we begin to feel an awakening through this inquiry. We naturally take moments of our day in deep contemplation to listen within. We notice that there is a witnessing of life that is cultivated through stillness. This witnessing becomes a powerful guide post, as in the very witnessing we experience a profound transformation.

This witnessing is love; it is willingness, it is a return to truth.

The Kingdom is within, a place of deep rest and Peace. This is where we journey to find true and lasting healing and the awakening of infinite love within our heart.

The hand of a Divine presence is always guiding us inward to the truth of being.

Within our fractures the light enters, deepening our connection to our Source. It is here we experience the evolution of love within our soul. Our life lessons become gifts of grace and we allow the pain of life to take us deeper into the silent, untouched aspect of our heart.

There is a gift of a miracle in our broken hearts.

The acceptance of this gift by our soul is the beginning of union with the Divine. Through taking our rightful place as a child of God, we open our hearts to receive. We experience a profound state of gratitude and we offer our life as a prayer of service to the work of the Holy Spirit.

Compassion blossoms through tending to the garden of our soul.

Key of Light

Through forgiveness, the act of letting go, giving love to oneself and others,
we raise our frequency to the Divine vibration of compassion.
Compassion is the well spring of the heart and it flowers through forgiveness.

The End of Illusions

Forgive us our illusions, Father, and help us to accept our true relationship with You,

in which there are no illusions, and where none can ever enter.

Our holiness is Yours.

What can there be in us that NEEDS forgiveness when Yours is perfect?

The sleep of forgetfulness is only the unwillingness to remember

Your forgiveness and Your Love.

Let us not wander into temptation,

for the temptation of the Son of God is not Your Will.

And let us receive only what YOU have given,

and accept but this into the minds which You created,

and which You love.

Amen.

Course in Miracles

Attaining Inner Peace is the most cherished and cared for
accomplishment of every Individual.

Sri Sri Adi Shankaracharya

Letting go gives us freedom,
and freedom is the only condition for happiness.
If in our heart we still cling to anything - anger, anxiety, or possessions -
we cannot be free.

Thich Nhat Hanh

Letting Go ~
Receive the Light of God

Within you lives the capacity to receive the immense love and light of God. When the content of your consciousness holds so much memory from the past it becomes an energetic barrier to receive this Divine grace. The stories that are held within, form a fictitious sense of self, along with the accumulation of judgments about your life experience. Your sense of self is veiled through a curtain of good, bad, right, wrong, regret, and so forth.

Look deep within and you will realize your inner self that is free from outward experiences and has been a witness to your life all along.

Through the release of the content of your experience, you receive the light of God. This is when the true healing begins and you walk the path of freedom and Peace.

Peace becomes a choice every day that you give yourself as a child of God.

Through the consciousness of separation, the ego self resists letting go as it means the end of its false identification. It holds on to the patterns of suffering and thrives off the mind-made sense of self to keep it alive.

Begin now to deepen your inner practice of Peace: the art of letting go.

Your life stories weave joy and sorrow within your soul but you cannot be defined by these stories. The real and untouched "you" lives deeper within your Sacred heart; uncovered by the practice of letting go.

The work of your beautiful heart is one of integration and compassion.

Letting go frees your heart so it can do its Sacred work. Your life stories with all its joys and sorrows can then be integrated in the context of your soul's journey of awakening. Then the gifts of your precious life may be received.

Your heart may receive all the love, gratitude and wisdom gained from the stories of your life.

Key of Light

Deep within your soul there is a temple of eternal light.

This light is not dependent on your ego. It is independent of the world.

Letting go of any separation from God is the first step

to uncovering the eternal light within.

Sacred Practice

Letting Go

Seek only the truth in your life and you will transcend the illusion of the world. Through seeking the truth, the light of the Divine shines on your path guiding you home. When you yearn for the truth, you will naturally let go of the content of your consciousness so that you may be filled with the presence of the Holy Spirit.

The light within you is the light as God. This light will set you free.
The light within you will guide you on your path of transcendence.

Simply ask, and you shall receive.

Let go,
Let God.

The treasure I have found
cannot be described in words,
the mind cannot conceive of it.

Adi Shankara

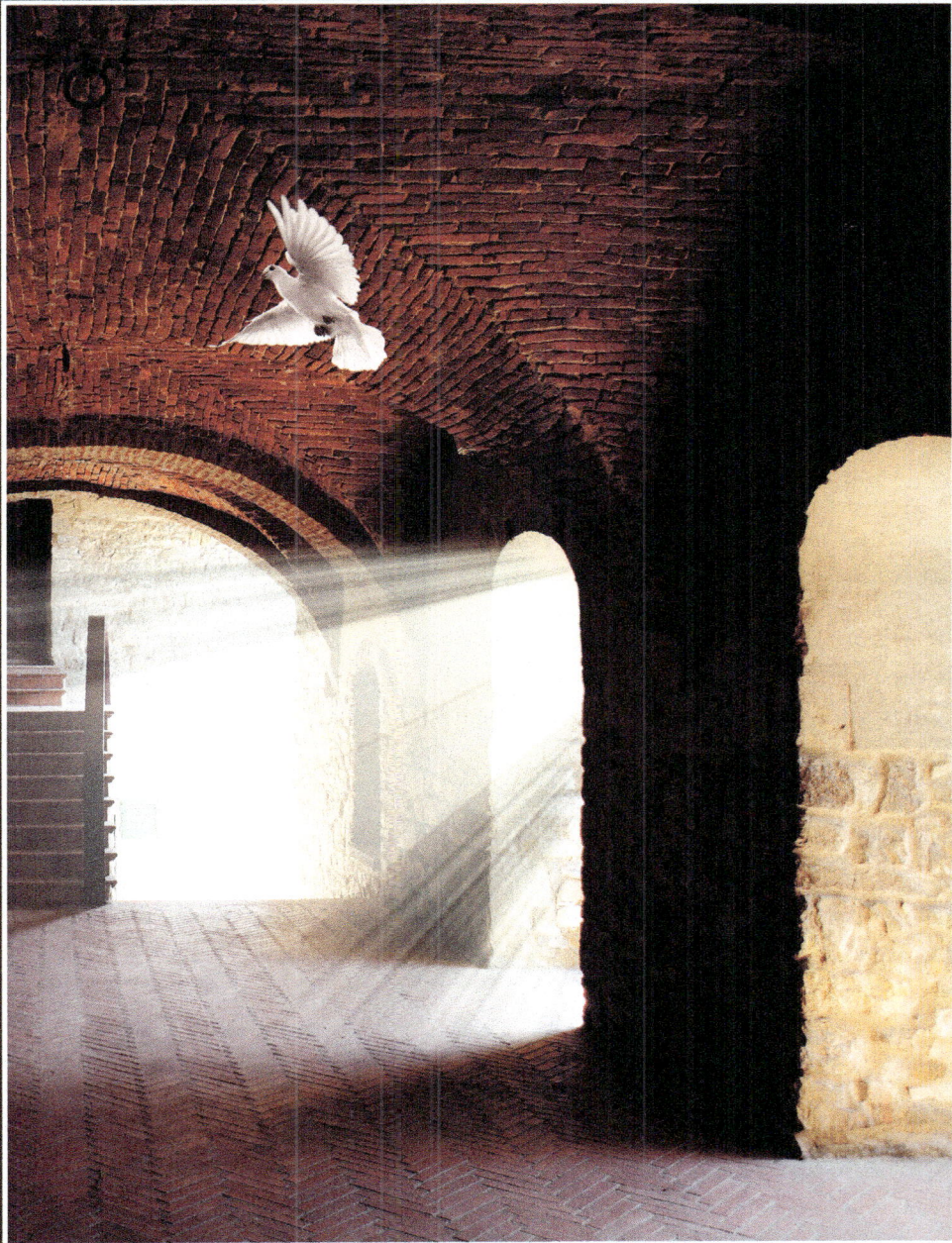

Forgiveness is part of the treasure you need to craft your falcon
wings and return to your true realm of Divine freedom.

Hafiz

Being in the Miracle Moment

Have you ever wondered about the miracle of life? The simple miracle of the breath? A miracle is the immense grace of being wherein your soul has infinite capacity to love, to learn, and to keep expanding into unlimited potential.

Each moment is a miracle of life; the gift of life that your soul has received.

There is a great love that is behind all of manifestation, so profound you need only step into the still point of your heart to experience its vastness. When you train your mind to enter the silent, unchanging nature of your Sacred heart, you give permission for Divine Consciousness to act in your life.

This is an invitation to the miracle.

Through resting in your Sacred heart, you will experience the miracle of being. Your mind when silent will become a tool for miracles to act in your life.

Invite your mind to rest in Peace. Within your Peace, a portal to God opens as you ascend into the light of your Divine being.

This true Divine Consciousness has no beginning or end. It is the stream of light that runs through the core of your being. This vertical, pillar-like energy connects you deeply within life's manifestation and meets the highest aspect of yourself.

Key of Light

Miracles come from your Divine Source where all your needs are met.

In your rest, in your silent practice of communion,

you enter the wellspring of your Sacred energy.

Miracles occur naturally as expressions of love.
The real miracle is the love that inspires them.
In this sense everything that comes from love
is a miracle.

Course in Miracles

The Divine Chalice-
An Offering to Serve

The Chalice is metaphor for our soul. When we are empty, free of afflictions from the past or worry about the future we are able to invite the Sacred light of the Divine to fill us with love, light and Peace.

When our intention is set to serve God, rather then serve our ego nature, we become a conduit of healing light and offer that light to the world.

We live the question, "How can I serve?" and listen to Divine guidance.

This way of being leads us to our life purpose; our true Sacred calling.

When we open our hearts and allow God to fill our inner chalice we are gifted with the eternal Peace and joy of being.

We bless the world with our light,
we heal the world with our love.

Become totally empty.
Quiet the restlessness of the mind.
Only then will you witness everything unfolding from emptiness.

Lao Tzu

Key of Light

Deep inside your Sacred Heart is the living presence of the Divine.
This Holy force, when activated, will heal your energy body
and you will experience a rebirth of your consciousness;
one that is free from the bondage of the mind.

Your Divine Chalice

Your Divine chalice is your temple body, graced with God's healing light. Open to this higher force by releasing what is untrue in your life.

Through your emptiness, you will be filled with the light of the Holy Spirit and you will be used in service to the awakening consciousness.

The first proof God's presence is an ineffable Peace.
This evolves into joy humanly inconceivable.
Once you have touched the Source of truth and life,
all nature will respond to you.
Finding God within, you will find Him without,
in all people and all conditions.

Paramahansa Yogananda

Chalice Prayer

Father ~
to Thee I raise my whole being,
a vessel emptied of self.
Accept Lord ~ this my emptiness and so fill me
with Thyself ~ Thy light, Thy Love, Thy Life ~
that these Thy Precious Gifts may radiate through me
and overflow the chalice of my heart into the hearts
of all with whom I come into contact this day,
revealing unto them the beauty of Thy Joy
and Wholeness and the serenity of Thy Peace,
which nothing can destroy.

Frances Nuttall

Sacred Practice

Living in The Truth

Each day is a new day to live in the truth of your being. Each day, you can begin anew without the context of the past.

Freedom becomes the very breath you breathe and you
live your life as a light in the world. This way of being is your natural state.

Truth is always new, therefore timeless.

What was truth yesterday is not truth today,

what is truth today is not truth tomorrow: truth has no continuity.

It is the mind which wants to make the experience which it calls truth

continuous, and such a mind shall not know truth.

Truth is always new: it is to see the same smile and see that smile newly,

to see the same person and see that person anew,

to see the waving palms anew, to meet life anew.

J Krishnamurti

Only when human beings are able
to perceive and acknowledge
the Self in each other
can there be real Peace.

Sri Mata Amritanandamayi

Open to the truth and the truth will set you free.

The Rose Within Your Heart

The rose represents the flowering of Sacred love within your heart.

It is through your devotion to God, that your inner rose opens and the fragrance of your Divine being is expressed.

The mystical journey of your soul is like a flowering rose. It is through your devotion to God, that your inner rose opens and the fragrance of your Divine being is expressed.

Through your inner flowering, your soul blossoms in the beauty of creation. This Holy opening within will guide you on the path of true service.

It is the flowering of consciousness within your Sacred heart that lifts your spirit beyond the dimension of sorrow into the realm of infinite love.

I will spend my heaven doing good upon the earth.
I will let fall a shower of roses.

St. Theresa of Lisieux

The Impersonal Life

The impersonal life is the way of freedom from sorrow. It is a choice that is made when the heart has broken open and there is little left of oneself to remain in the old way of being.

You live in each precious moment as if it were your last. Through your transcendence of personal identification, you ascend to a lighter sense of self, free from the burdens of the past.

Your heartbreak from the human realm leads you to commune with your Divine Source and you open to a greater light within. Through unity with the Divine, this light becomes your guidepost for your journey to the Kingdom.

You have to keep breaking your heart
until it opens.

Rumi

The Infinite Unfolding of Beauty

The beauty of your soul is celestial light expressing
through your heart. This light of your heart shines in
many colors of the rainbow of creation.

The beauty within you is a reflection of the
beauty of God.

The body again will become restless,
until your soul paints all the beauty upon the sky,
for when the heart tastes its glorious destiny and you awake.

Hafiz

The Mystical Portal

Journey deep within your Sacred heart and there you will embark upon a mystical portal that opens to your infinite being. This still point within is a most beautiful resting place; an inner refuge where you are restored to wholeness.

When you need renewal in body, mind and spirit, breathe deeply and let go into your Sacred heart. Allow your mind to be immersed in this most healing light.

This Divine light will guide you on your path, assisting you to let go of your identification with time, form and false sense of self.

When you open the mystical portal of your heart, you begin to ascend into a higher dimension of consciousness. You no longer identify with a personal sense of self; you understand that you are truly a spiritual being in a physical body.

In the heaven realms of your consciousness, you become one with the infinite Source. It is within this realm you receive the love, beauty and truth of your Divine heritage.

This healing love guides you to forgive the mistakes of the egoic personality and to release yourself from the bondage of karma on the earth plane.

The mystical portal to God opens through your surrender and you are lifted into the beloved's arms.

It is within this realm you receive the love, beauty and truth of your Divine heritage.

Key of Light
Listen to your inner calling
as it will lead you to the truth of your life's purpose;
a most Sacred work.

The unchangeable can only be realized in silence.
Once realized, it will deeply affect the changeable,
itself remaining unaffected.

Sri Nisargadatta Maharaj

Prayer
Communion with God

The human condition is one of survival with very little time to discover your Divine self. When you take a few moments each day to pause and breathe, you begin to live your life more consciously.

As a disciple of truth there is a willingness within to surrender your mind and rest in your Source.

Communion, a blessing of union with the Divine, softens your heart, and brings more joy to your spirit. Through this practice you will live your life in Peace, filled with love, truth and beauty.

Key of Light

Living your life as a prayer is the invocation to God
in which your heart opens and you receive the healing light
and love necessary for all areas of your life.

When you find Peace within yourself,
you become the kind of person
who can live at Peace with others.

Peace Pilgrim

Teach Us How To Pray

Oh Thou, from whom the breath of life comes,
Who fills all realms of sound,
light and vibration.
May Your light be experienced
in my utmost holiest.
Your Heavenly Domain approaches.
Let Your will come true -
in the universe (all that vibrates)
just as on earth (that is material and dense).
Give us wisdom (understanding, assistance)
for our daily need,
detach the fetters of faults that bind us, (karma)
like we let go the guilt of others.
Let us not be lost in superficial things
(materialism, common temptations),
but let us be freed from that which keeps us
from our true purpose.
From You comes the all-working will,
the lively strength to act,
the song that beautifies all and renews itself
from age to age.
Amen.
Sealed in trust, faith and truth.

The Lord's Prayer

Our Father in heaven,
hallowed be Your Name,
Your Kingdom come,
Your Will be done on earth as it is on heaven.
Give us today our daily bread,
forgive us our debts,

as we also have forgiven our debtors.
and lead us not into temptation,
but deliver us from the evil one.
For Yours is the Kingdom and the Power
and the Glory for ever.
Amen.

The Aramaic Prayer of Jesus
Lord's Prayer in Original Aramaic

Abwoon d'bvashmayo, nethqadash shmok.

Te-the malkutokh. Nehwé

tseby o-nokh, aykano d'bvash'mayo of -ba'r'o.

Habv lan lahma d'sunqonan

yow-mano, Washboqlan hawbén w'kh-t'hén, aykano

dof h'ran shba-qn l'hayobén.

W'lo tahlan l'nesyun'eh, elo patson men bisho.

Metol d'dilok hi malkutokh, w'haylo,

w'teshbuh-to lo'alam 'o-l'min.

Amén.

177

Sacred Practice
Communion With God

Love your life and life will reveal to you the secrets of the universe.

Love so deeply, that you hear the voice of God within.

This voice within is the light that guides you home.

This is the light of your being that will illuminate the darkness of the world.

With each breath of release, you relax deeper
and deeper into the temple of your Sacred heart.

When the light of Divine love permeates your heart and soul,
I swear, you will be more radiant than the sun.

Drown in the sea of God for a moment, and see
how the waters of the seven seas will not harm you.

From head to toe, you will become the light of God,
when you surrender your self to Divine glory.

When Divine grace becomes the focus of your gaze,
you will be exalted by the inner light of your vision.

Hafiz

*I wish I could show you, when you are lonely or in
darkness, the astonishing light of your own being.*

Hafiz

Witnessing

Mirroring The Sacred

Is it possible that the mind can function as a mirror for the Sacred? In a meditative state, your mind is still and in Peace. Your Sacred heart, when free from the bondage of your mind, is the very essence of intelligence.

It is from an empty mind that you mirror the Sacred in your life and you are guided home to the Kingdom. This profound art of witnessing is a way of being that opens your mind to a greater perception.

The Art of Witnessing

The inner work of the disciple of truth is to direct the mind into your Sacred heart. Through dissolving the mind into your heart you will experience a profound sense of unity with God. Mirroring the Sacred becomes the art of your soul as you realize it is through witnessing you are aligned with the highest love possible. This Sacred love will heal and transform what is seen.

The gift of witnessing is a profound self love that will heal and transform your life.

Empty yourself of everything.
Let the mind rest at Peace.
The ten thousand things rise and fall while the Self watches their return.
They grow and flourish and then return to the Source.
Returning to the Source is stillness,
which is the way of nature.

Lao Tzu

Key of Light

The gift of witnessing will become your
key to well-being in both mind and Spirit.
Sanctify your life by becoming a vessel of Divine light.

Unity with Source

In truth, you are never separated from your Source. The illusion of separation appears from layers and layers of conditioning that has developed an untrue sense of self.

Within you lives the eternal presence of God; this presence reveals that you are a spark of light in the world. This light shines brightly through the evolution of love within your soul.

When you are identified with yourself as a separate individual, you may experience a feeling of numbness in your spirit that is the result of the identification with your personal self. This is the cause of great sorrow.

When you are free to be yourself, you dance in the beauty and joy of creation. As a child of God there is a humbleness of your spirit. The innocence of your true nature allows you to receive Divine guidance for your journey home.

When you let go of your personal identity, you naturally meet the formless essence of your true nature.

It is through quiet moments of communion and prayer, you touch into the infinite ocean of being. This is the wellspring of your soul where you experience unity with the Divine.

Key of Light

Within you dwells the living presence of God.
This Sacred Source is the very breath you breathe.
In quiet contemplation, when you rest in stillness
you have access to this beautiful stream of Divine light.

"You see what you choose to see,
because all perception is a choice.
And when you cease to impose your meanings on what you see,
your spiritual eyes will open,
and you will see a world free of judgment
and shining in its endless beauty.

Paul Ferrini

Love is Presence

To feel the Love of God within you is to see the world anew,
shining in innocence, alive with hope, and blessed with perfect charity and love.

Course in Miracles

When you contemplate the truth of love, you may witness that personal love is what you have known through time and memory. Personal love is one that holds the memories of the past and will attract new experiences to heal the wounds of the heart. This love often is an expression of the surface heart. In your deeper heart, your soul has the infinite capacity to evolve into an unconditional love that is eternal and free from the past. When you reach deep within your heart you will discover a love that is beyond personal love; a love that is founded in compassion, truth and beauty.

When Love is Presence it expresses as the willingness to give of your spirit
to each new moment of your day. This is the beauty of a soul whose life is in devotion
to the evolution of love for all of humanity.

When Love is Presence there is awareness; an action of seeing the truth
and there is no fear about what is being seen.

When Love is Presence it brings the gift of transformation to your life;
this most Sacred love attends to what needs healing without thought.
Love transcends thought and guides your mind to rest in your Sacred heart.

When Love is Presence it is pure goodness;
transcending ego identification through forgiveness and compassion.

When Love is Presence there is a great intention to live in harmlessness;
all actions are filtered through the consciousness of love.

When Love is Presence there is an ability to have great compassion for
life's experiences in this suffering world.

Love is Presence and within this consciousness of love you live in service. You are guided to offer a hand of love and kindness to all who need. You join the circle of light to assist the awakening love within all humanity.

I want that love that is the silence of Eternity.

Rumi

Sacred Practice

Be a Beacon of Light

*D*eep within your heart lives the infinite light of God guiding you to the Kingdom. Spend moments of your day to rest in this most peaceful light.

This light will restore you to the beauty of your true essence. This light will reveal the truth of your being.

You are destined to become a beacon of light, to serve this suffering world, offering others a helping hand along the way.

In your sacred practice, you will soon realize the love and light within your heart is directly activated through prayer and stillness.

Your true abiding nature is simply light, you are the light of the world.

In your light you join the community of awakening souls to heal the sorrow of humanity.

Be a light unto yourself; betake yourselves to no external refuge.
Hold fast to the Truth. Look not for refuge to anyone besides yourselves.

Buddha Shakyamuni

Heaven is Within You

When you open to Divine love, you enter the heaven realm of your being.

Heaven is a place in your consciousness where you are invited to put thought to rest, and experience the Peace of God.

Within the realm of heaven lives your true essence of light. This light illuminates your path home.

Heaven is a state of being in which you are no longer controlled by your mind. Your mind is surrendered to the light within your heart.

The inner light of your heart is the doorway to the heaven realm. God opens this doorway through your silence and surrendered prayer.

In Silence, you enter heaven's gate.

Key of Light

A flowering lotus blossoms within your heart,
each unfolding petal represents the awakening of truth,
beauty and love within you.
The keys to the Kingdom of heaven are revealed
through your hearts surrender to your Holy Source.

Ask, Seek, Knock
Ask and it will be given to you;
Seek and you will find;
Knock and the door will be opened to you.

Matthew 7:7

Remember,
the entrance door to the sanctuary is inside you.

Rumi

Living in Beauty

Beauty is a Divine expression: the light entering the eyes of a child, the compassion one feels for the suffering of humankind, the incredible manifestation of the natural world. Beauty is seen in all things good, within and without. In a Divine state of beauty, you are surrendered to life's changing appearance and you see the truth among what is changing.

Beauty is your inner harmony with the outer world.

It is the grace of being that is the background of all your experiences. Timeless and untouched, the light of Divine beauty is your gift from God.

Beauty is the essence of your soul.

You are an unfolding flower with the fragrance of the Divine, your soul's exquisite perfume.

Let the beauty of what you love
be what you do.

Rumi

The man who lives without conflict,
who lives with beauty and love,
is not frightened of death
because to love is to die.

J Krishnamurti

Sacred Practice

Tending to the Garden of Your Soul

The garden within your soul is the most beautiful of God's Creation. The flowers of kindness, love, compassion, beauty, and joy are the result of tending to your soul's garden.

The garden within your soul is worthy of great care. Love your soul as you are a child of God. When your ego-self feels negative emotions such as judgement, shame, or anger, turn your attention into your heart and surrender all self-inflictions to God.

Your true nature will transform feelings that cause you unhappiness into beautiful blossoms of Spirit.

Through deep surrender and allowing the Divine to fill your heart you will unify with the Sacred essence of your soul.

To know yourself as the Being underneath the thinker,
the stillness underneath the mental noise,
the love and joy underneath the pain,
is freedom, salvation, enlightenment.

Eckhart Tolle

Gratitude – a Way of Being

When unified with your Source, gratitude for life's blessings becomes a natural aspect of your consciousness. When the ego identity is dissolved, what remains is your true nature as a spark of the Divine. No longer feeling separation, you see yourself as a part of all of life and you walk in grace with deep gratitude.

Gratitude is the heart's ability to feel the miracle of life and is the expression of the soul who understands that life is a gift from God.

To be grateful is to recognize the Love of God
in everything He has given us -
and He has given us everything.
Every breath we draw is a gift of His love,
every moment of existence is a grace,
for it brings with it immense graces from Him.
Gratitude therefore takes nothing for granted,
is never unresponsive, is constantly awakening to new wonder
and to praise of the goodness of God.
For the grateful person knows that God is good,
not by hearsay, but by experience.
And that is what makes all the difference.

Thomas Merton

Sacred Practice

Seek the Source From Which all Things Come

The missing link in most humans is that their souls are deprived of love. From this state there is a lack of gratitude. What is given is often expected, so humans are never really grateful. There is an illness of entitlement in society, leading to great violence and wars. This entitlement virus is affecting children from an early age and causing more brutality in our world.

The use of the term "gratitude" has become a cliché, an affirmation of the mind.

Deeper than the idea of gratitude lives a separate self who is only focused on self-gain. This self-gain leads to affirming gratitude for what one has attained. Leading to a mind-made sense of gratitude. Who are you within the Peace of your heart? This inquiry is an essential step in your awakening.

Within your heart. Take a close look to see if your heart is pure. You will notice the "I" self there. Observe this aspect of your being and see if it is actively grasping or in a desire state.

When there is an observation of grasping or desiring it can be an invitation to look and see who is it that is seeking?

Seek the Source from which all things come. When you commune with the Source within your heart all of life appears as a blessing.

Gratitude is the fairest blossom
which springs from the soul.
Rumi

The Transformation of Self

The wisdom to discern the real from the unreal is a
requirement on your path to God realization.

The path to God is one of unity, not duality.

The inner work of the seeker of truth is to see clearly that the world
is a manifestation of the human condition. This condition is the
product of ill thinking. To become free from this illness, you must see
the world without an investment of self-identity. You must be ready
to see the world without yourself in the picture.

*The transformation of Self occurs when you can live
without the parameters of the world's conditioning.
This way of being is your soul's truth.*

Opening Your Celestial Energy Body

The most important healing comes from the light of your celestial energy field also known as the causal body. In this dimension, Divine frequencies are transmitted through the language of light.

When there is healing from the soul plane or celestial level of consciousness, you will experience a feeling of lightness and elevation of your spiritual vibration. You will feel a greater alignment with your truth and the present moment becomes alive with joy and well-being.

Your light body awakens through letting go of thought and emotions that keep you bound to separation. The yearning to meet your true nature will guide you to let go of the identification with your mind and open the doorway to your innermost heart; the light of your being.

Key of Light

When you spend moments of your day in silence or meditation,
you open to Divine frequencies and they are transmitted
and become integrated in your energy body.
You experience a greater vitality and joy.

Man is spirit—that is all man needs to know:
and spirit is triumphant over matter.

White Eagle

Sacred Practice

Choose God

You may believe that you are responsible for what you do,
but not for what you think.
The truth is that you are responsible for what you think,
because it is only at this level that you can exercise choice.
What you do comes from what you think.

Marianne Williamson

In life there are times when the challenges are great. This is the time when you must choose God.

In every experience God is holding your hand; and you must also choose to hold the hand of God.

This life is so very short, and will be over before you are able to know your true purpose. This is your urgent call for your soul's awakening.

Time is only for the realization of God. Take time to heal the mind of separation and to unify with the Holy Spirit.

The Holy Spirit guides you, protects you, and embraces you on your path of return. Through surrender you are carried on the wings of grace to the Kingdom.

Your path will show you the wisdom needed for your soul's awakening, and will heal the wounds of separation.

Seek the Kingdom first and you will be restored to wholeness.

You are within God. God is within you.

Peace Pilgrim

When you are inspired by some great purpose,
some extraordinary project, all your thoughts break their bonds:
Your mind transcends limitations, your consciousness expands
in every direction, and you find yourself in a new, great and
wonderful world. Dormant forces, faculties and talents become
alive, and you discover yourself to be a greater person by far
than you ever dreamed yourself to be.

Patañjali

If you are depressed, you are living in the past.
If you are anxious, you are living in the future.
If you are at Peace, you are living in the present.

Lao Tzu

The End of Fear

Through entering the inner sanctuary of your heart you will let go of your separate sense of self and dissolve the thought patterns that hold you in fear. You will understand that there is no death, as your eternal being cannot die. The only ending is the accumulated identity that has formed a false sense of self. The more identification with the false self, the more fear there is in one's life and the fear of losing one's life. What dies is this false sense of self.

The Divine truth is that you are life, you do not have life and you will never lose life. You are the miracle of eternal life. It is within stillness that you are able to perceive the formless dimension of your being; the living, eternal, witness consciousness that has always been presiding over your life.

Welcome the precious moments in your life when you are able to commune with your eternal spirit; a time of joyous being. In your joy, in your rest, you will know the Source from which all things come.

Peace is the vehicle to awaken to the infinite love and light of your sacred soul;
a path of remembrance.

Death is a stripping away of all that is not you.
The secret of life is to "die before you die" and find that there is no death.
Eckhart Tolle

Key of Light

There is no end to life for you are life.
The eternal light that will always shine, with or without form.

I didn't come here of my own accord,
and I can't leave that way.
Whoever brought me here will have to take me home.

Jalaluddin Mevlana Rumi

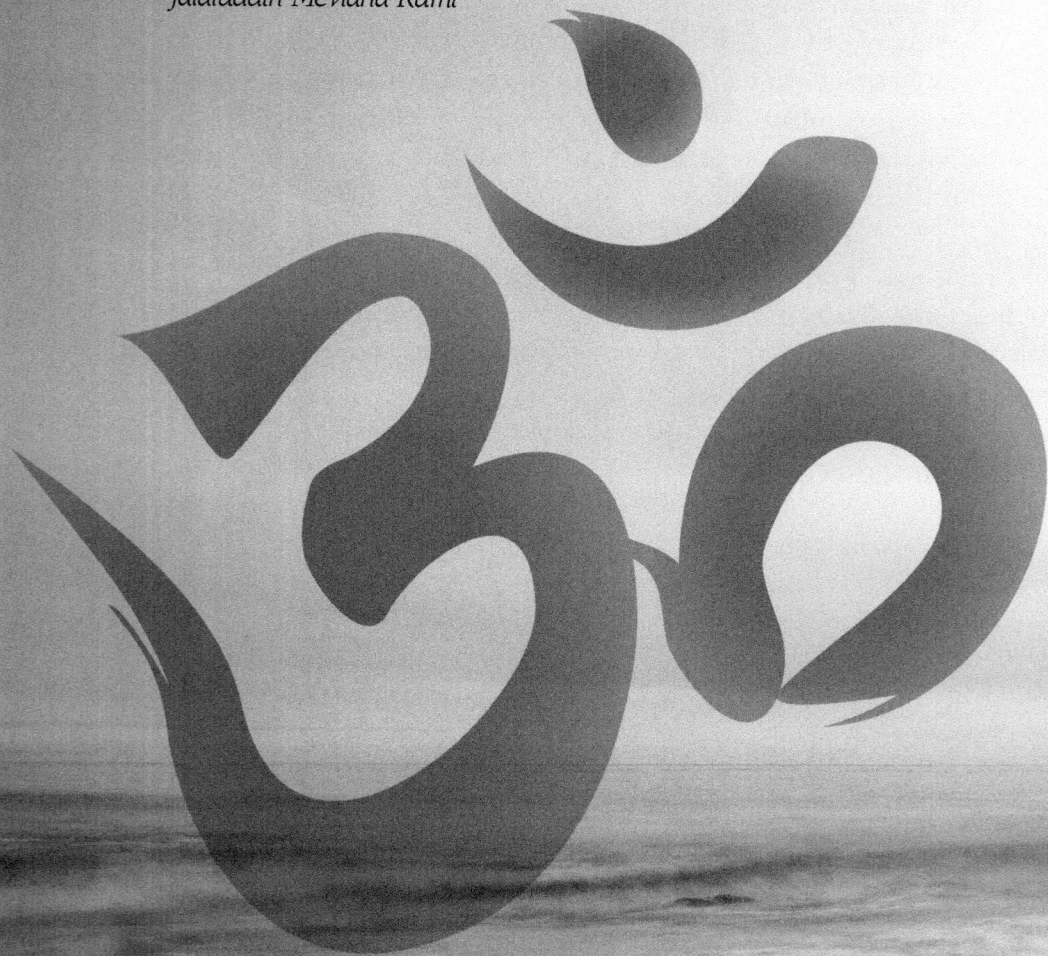

Shanti or Peace Mantra

The "sarveshaam mantra" is one of the Peace or shanti mantras
which may be used to invoke harmony and tranquility.

AUM sarveshaam svastir bhavatu,
sarveshaam shaantir bhavatu
sarveshaam poornam bhavatu,
sarveshaam mangalam bhavatu
sarve bhavantu sukhinah,
sarve santu niraamayaah
sarve bhadraani pashyantu,
maa kashchidh dukh bhaag-bhavet.

Meaning of the Sarveshaam Shanti Mantra

Let it be so ordained that all the people experience
well-being; let all the people experience Peace or tranquility.
Let all the people experience wholeness and completeness;
let them experience prosperity and auspiciousness.
May it so happen that everyone receives happiness.

The Eternal Light of the Soul

Within you lives an untouched, eternal light. This most loving light offers you an inner refuge where you can turn to receive strength and wisdom to walk the path of your highest good.

In the world of maya or illusion you often forget this most Sacred light and walk in darkness. You experience the sorrows of the world: birth, old age, sickness and death without the context of your spiritual awakening.

Your inner light is the guidepost and beacon within your soul, where you receive healing for your body, mind and spirit. It is your light body that is strengthened through the evolution of love within your heart. Your light body is the "star" of your highest potential and the five points of the star represent your soul's gifts.

Your soul's gifts are the radiant Divine rays that you uniquely offer back to your Creator through service.

You become a star in God's creation and will form light codes that assist in the evolution of Peace, truth and love.

Here is, in truth, the whole secret of Yoga,
the science of the soul.
The active turnings, the strident vibrations,
of selfishness, lust and hate are to be stilled by
meditation, by letting heart and mind dwell in
spiritual life, by lifting up the heart to the strong,
silent life above, which rests in the stillness of
eternal love, and needs no harsh vibration
to convince it of true being.

Patañjali

Oh! Listen,

I will sing to thee the song of my Beloved.

Where the soft green slopes of the still mountains

Meet the blue shimmering waters of the noisy sea,

Where the bubbling brook shouts in ecstasy,

Where the still pools reflect the calm heavens,

There thou wilt meet with my Beloved.

In the vale where the cloud hangs in loneliness

Searching the mountain for rest,

In the still smoke climbing heavenwards,

In the hamlet toward the setting sun,

In the thin wreaths of the fast disappearing clouds,

There thou wilt meet with my Beloved.

Among the dancing tops of the tall cypress,

Among the gnarled trees of great age,

Among the frightened bushes that cling to the earth,

Among the long creepers that hang lazily,

There thou wilt meet with my Beloved.

In the ploughed fields where noisy birds are feeding,

On the shaded path that winds along the full, motionless river,

Beside the banks where the waters lap,

Amidst the tall poplars that play ceaselessly with the winds,

In the dead tree of last summer's lightning,

There thou wilt meet with my Beloved.

In the still blue skies,

Where heaven and earth meet

In the breathless air,

In the morn burdened with incense,

Among the rich shadows of a noon-day,

Among the long shadows of an evening,

Amidst the gay and radiant clouds of the setting sun,

On the path on the waters at the close of the day,

There thou wilt meet with my Beloved.

In the shadows of the stars,

In the deep tranquility of dark nights,

In the reflection of the moon on still waters,

In the great silence before the dawn,

Among the whispering of waking trees,

In the cry of the bird at morn,

Amidst the wakening of shadows,

Amidst the sunlit tops of the far mountains,

In the sleepy face of the world,

There thou wilt meet with my Beloved.

Keep still, O dancing waters,

And listen to the voice of my Beloved.

In the happy laughter of children

Thou canst hear Him.

The music of the flute Is His voice.

The startled cry of a lonely bird

Moves thy heart to tears,

For thou hearest His voice.

The roar of the age-old sea

Awakens the memories

That have been lulled to sleep

By His voice.

The soft breeze that stirs

The tree-tops lazily

Brings to thee the sound

Of His voice.

The thunder among the mountains

fills thy soul

With the strength

Of His voice.

In the roar of a vast city,

through the voices of the night,

The cry of sorrow,

The shout of joy,

Through the ugliness of anger,

Comes the voice of my Beloved.

In the distant blue isles,

On the soft dewdrop,

On the breaking wave,

On the sheen of waters,

On the wing of the flying bird,

On the tender leaf of the spring,

Thou wilt see the face of my Beloved.

In the Sacred temple,

In the halls of dancing,

On the Holy face of the sannyasi,

In the lurches of the drunkard,

With the harlot and with the chaste,

Thou wilt meet with my Beloved.

On the fields of flowers,

In the towns of squalor and dirt,

With the pure and the unholy,

In the flower that hides divinity,

There is my well-Beloved.

Oh! the sea has entered my heart,

In a day,

I am living a hundred summers.

O, friend,

I behold my face in thee,

The face of my well-Beloved.

This is the song of my love.

J. Krishnamurti

Soul Transformation
The Path to Peace

You find Peace not by rearranging the circumstances of your life,
but by realizing who you are at the deepest level.
Eckhart Tolle

Nothing is more important than your soul's transformation, as you are only in this life for God. As a child you were unified with God and lived in the natural joy of Divine presence. And, then the mind developed and soon this presence receded into the background.

Soul transformation is returning to your original light and choosing each moment from this Divine Consciousness.

The Holy presence of God has always been with you. Through presence you are restored to wholeness. Through presence you release the past. Open your heart to this Holy presence that is always with you, and you will know Peace.

Seek the Kingdom first and you will realize the truth of your life. It is through this yearning for God, that your inner doorway to heaven opens.

Your soul, when ready to unify with God, will guide you to open your heart and turn within to the light of your being. The first step to God is this turning.

With a surrendered mind and an open heart, the light of God is ignited within your soul.

The light of God provides a map of return, guiding you back to your Source of infinite love.

The secret of harmonious living
is the development of spiritual Consciousness.
In that consciousness, fear and anxiety disappear,
and life becomes meaningful with fulfillment as its keynote.

Joel Goldsmith

*The wisdom of your soul awakens through unity
with your true essence; the light within that is
guiding you home on the path of Grace.*

Always bear this in mind:
Everything is in God's hands,
and you are His tool to be used by Him as He pleases.
Try to grasp the significance of 'all is His'
and you will immediately feel free from all burdens.
What will be the result of your surrender to Him?
None will seem alien, all will be your very own Self.

Sri Anandamayi Ma

Sacred Practice

Soul Transformation

Begin each day with a prayer of surrender. Set your intention to be in Peace and allow your heart to release accumulated sorrow, worry and worldly concerns.

The Kingdom is within you. It is a place of deep Peace and rest. Spend precious moments in this Sacred place within and you will know God.

The wisdom of your soul awakens through unity with your true essence guiding you home on the path of Grace.

The kingdom of God is within us; the whole of the Godhead is to be found within our individual being, not in Holy mountains nor yet in the temple at Jerusalem, but within us.

Joel S. Goldsmith

Your prayer will not be an asking or a seeking
for any thing; it will be an asking and a seeking
and a knocking for more light, greater spiritual
wisdom, greater discernment.

Joel S. Goldsmith

This is what you are to do:

Lift your heart up to God,
with a gentle stirring of love desiring God for God's own sake and not for any gifts.
Center all your attention and desire on God
and let this be the sole concern of your mind and heart.
Do all in your power to forget everything else....
And so diligently persevere in it until you feel joy in it.
For in the beginning it is usual to feel nothing
but a kind of darkness about your mind,
as it were, a cloud of unknowing.
You will seem to know nothing and to feel nothing,
except a naked intent toward God in the depths of your being.
Try as you might, this darkness and cloud will remain between you and your God.
You will feel frustrated, for your mind will be unable to grasp God,
and your heart will not relish the delight of God's love.
But, learn to be at home in this darkness.
Return to it as often as you can,
letting your Spirit cry out to God whom you love.
For if, in this life, you hope to feel and see God as God is...
it must be within this darkness and this cloud.
But, if you strive to fix your love on God forgetting all else,
which is the work of contemplation I have urged you to begin,
I am confident that God in goodness will bring you to a deep experience of Godself....

If you want to gather all your desire into one simple word that the mind can easily retain,
choose a short word rather than a long one.
A one-syllable word such as "God" or "love" is best.
But, choose one that is meaningful to you.
Then fix it in your mind so that it will remain in there come what may.
This word will be your defense in conflict and in Peace....

As I have already explained to you,
this simple work is not a rival to your daily activities.
For with your attention centered on the blind awareness
of your naked being united to God's
you will go about your daily rounds, eating and drinking, sleeping and waking,
going and coming, speaking and listening, lying down and rising up, standing
and kneeling, running and riding, working and resting.
In the midst of it all, you will be offering to God continually each day
the most precious gift you can make.
This work will be at the heart of everything you do,
whether active or contemplative.

Anonymous—The Cloud of Unknowing

The Transcendent Path

Living in Heaven's Embrace

The Transcendent Path - Sacred Wisdom is the life work of Jaya Sarada based on the material from *The Sacred Path of Love-Communion with God* and *The Sacred Path of Peace-Keys to the Kingdom*, by Jaya Sarada. These offerings, retreats and webinars are intended to bring wisdom and healing, and contribute to the awakening of love that is so needed in our world.

Join us in invocation of the Sacred and Communion with God as we deepen our understanding of our true nature through stillness, meditation, movement and sacred inquiry.

Our gatherings are founded in the vibration of God that holds the principles of Love, Truth, and Beauty. We will share in our commitment to raise consciousness through the Holy medicine of Peace and service.

For more information on our gatherings and webinars or to learn about Jaya Sarada's work, please visit her at TheTranscendentPath.com.

For more information contact:
Jaya Sarada
1.855.505.3935
TheTranscendentPath.com
info@thetranscendentpath.com

10% of all proceeds will go to Divine Light Foundation which provides ministerial counseling and women's support.

CPSIA information can be obtained
at www.ICGtesting.com
Printed in the USA
BVOW11s0953130218
507465BV00006B/2/P